CHOICE FROM AMERICA
modern American ceramics

Arthur C. Danto
Janet Koplos

The Kruithuis Museums Collection, 's-Hertogenbosch/NL

CHOICE FROM AMERICA

modern American ceramics

CONTENTS

FOREWORD

If 'exaggeration' is typical of much American art in the second half of the 20th century, then ceramics is no exception. Enlargement or extreme minimisation, doubling, multiplying or else reducing, rendering banal or sublimating – one thing or the other, but nothing in between. This longing for extremes appears to have been the preferred strategy for American artists seeking to evade convention.

'Exaggeration' was certainly the most striking feature to emerge during any exploratory tour of the workshops of American clay artists in the early 1980s. European ceramics at that time remained very much a craft in the traditional mould. What we found in the US seemed like a revolution in comparison. The Americans totally shattered the best European and Asian ceramic tradition – so fiercely championed by people like Bernard Leach. They battered, stabbed, smashed and distorted the clay, the bottoms fell out of their dishes, the handles and lids flew off and the pot exploded: it was clearly art that we were witnessing.

The excitement of this experience prompted the exhibition 'Who's afraid of American Pottery?' (1983), which marked the inception of Museum Het Kruithuis's collection of US ceramics. The exhibition was like a bomb going off – the European public was simply not used to so much colour, so much brutality or to such an unorthodox approach to the medium of clay. Each new exhibition imbued with the pioneering spirit of American clay art sparked the same kind of sensation. From a retrospective of 'The Mad Potter of Biloxi, George Ohr (1857–1918)' to the work of Betty Woodman (1930), we were continually astonished by the form and colour.

In the meantime, Museum Het Kruithuis's collection of American ceramics has grown into the most substantial in Europe. It focuses explicitly on the 'container' form rather than on sculptural ceramics or installations. There are both pragmatic and fundamental reasons for this. Pragmatic, in that Het Kruithuis's existing collection of modern European ceramics is marked by the pot form, making the American collection a logical formal extension, while the contrasts between the two continents throw the collections into relief. At a more fundamental level, it was felt that the choice of the container form would help us to present the art historical development within the overall ceramics collection with greater clarity. After all, every development in the form and content of modern ceramics can be read from the container form.

This publication presents and describes Museum Het Kruithuis's entire collection of American ceramics for the first time. The aim is not only to present a catalogue for experts in the field – American ceramics is so fascinating and the vitality of the clay artists so infectious that this book ought to appeal to anyone who is at all interested in this marvellous art form.

Yvònne G.J.M. Joris
Director Museum Het Kruithuis

BETWEEN UTENSIL AND ART:
THE ORDEAL OF AMERICAN CERAMICS

Arthur C. Danto

There is a significant portion of the craft world for which the antonym of "craft" would not so much be "art", as the continuing controversy over the relationship between art and craft might suggest, but "industry". On this usage, craft refers to pre-industrial methods of producing objects of use and of embellishment, though no one who practiced craft in the pre-industrial world could have known that it was pre-industrial: "craft" could have had no special meaning when every item of human use was shaped by hand. But when many of these began to be produced by industrial processes – cloth, crockery and hand-tools themselves – craft became a self-conscious activity and implied a form of cultural criticism. In identifying oneself as a craftsperson one implicitly took a stand, articulated by John Ruskin and William Morris, against the culture of the Machine, declaring allegiance to earlier and less alienating forms of life. The founders of Arts and Crafts Movement of the late 1880s sought not only to recreate the principles of medieval facture, but to live, so far as possible, the forms of life in which their crafts belonged. We still see signs of this in the characteristic wares displayed at craft-fairs everywhere – the hand-loomed, the hand-wrought, the hand-woven, the hand-made, the hand-blown, the home-spun. These may serve the same domestic functions as their mass-produced counterparts, but their use ritualizes these functions and colors the consciousness of those who use them. As when, to take an extreme instance, the participant in a tea ceremony holds the tea bowl up for contemplation – a gesture presumably inappropriate were the bowl mass-produced.

In this sense, much of contemporary craft has less in common than it does with the art of our times. This exposes its practitioners to criticism from both sides, which has been especially so in the world of ceramics. From the one side, ceramists who aspire to art are held to have forsaken the traditional system of uses in which such objects as plates and beakers, platters and bowls, derive meanings that are partly moral and partly aesthetic. From the other side, an almost metaphysical boundary between craft and art has often been insisted upon by artists, particularly in America, for whom "craft" has at times been a critically dismissive term, like "decorative" or "literary" or "illustrational". Ceramists who aspire to the status of artist are accordingly like persons without a country, defined by a double rejection. In terms of actual praxis, they must have acquired the same skills as those whose goals they have in some way abandoned. But the abandonment of those goals does not as such enfranchise them as citizens of the art world. An unmistakable interest, however, attaches to objects which occupy this uneasy zone between pots and paintings, not entirely craft yet not entirely art, much in the way in which human beings have been thought of as occupying an anomalous station between animals and angels – disturbing a cosmic order in which each thing has its place. The question this hybrid form of being raises is what must be added to ceramic praxis to make it art – unless indeed the very terms of that praxis are incompatible with something being art. This will be the topic of this essay.

Craft-work was assigned so elevated a meaning under the auspices of Arts and Crafts that to its adherents, it seemed that any distinction between it and fine art was arbitrary. In America, however, painting achieved an undeniable sublimity under Abstract Expressionism so disproportionate to what craft at its highest appeared capable, that the sense of a boundary between them re-emerged with an assertiveness it had not had since the days of High Romanticism. Abstract Expressionism was itself a late flowering of the Romantic spirit and the condescension it felt toward the crafts might be explained in part by glancing at the way the defining philosophies of Romanticism framed the distinction. It is worth examining, if but briefly, the place of art in the great philosophical systems of Kant and Hegel.

In his Critique of Judgment, Kant distinguished between free and dependent art [16]. The latter "is ascribed to objects which come under the concept of a particular purpose". Art is accordingly free when it does not come under such a concept and when, accordingly, it advances no individual interests. Dissociating free art from the category of purpose – Kant characterizes beauty as "purposive without any specific purpose" – the satisfaction such art affords can in principle be universal. Hence it can be the "symbol of morality", since moral principles, as Kant analyzed them, must be universalizable. But craft, in the Arts and Crafts sense, is dedicated specifically to objects with purposes so integral to their design that it is difficult to see how they could be free in the way art is when entirely dissociated from purpose.

Kant's distinction between "free" and "dependent" art is developed systematically by Hegel, in his tremendous Lectures on Aesthetics. It is central to Hegel's vision that art constitutes what he terms a "moment" of Absolute Spirit: art "only fulfils its supreme task when it has placed itself in the same sphere as religion and philosophy". It is one way of bringing to our minds "the deepest interests of mankind and the most comprehensive truths of the spirit". It "points through and beyond itself and itself hints at something spiritual of which it is to give us an idea". Hence art is a mode of the spirit's self-cognition, limited only by the fact that it presents its truths in sensuous terms. But Hegel is at pains to explain that he is speaking here of what he terms free art only. "It is of course the case that art can be used as a fleeting play, affording recreation and entertainment, decorating our surroundings, giving pleasantness to the externals of our life and making other objects stand out by artistic adornment". [7] In the broad sense of the term, art "intersperses with its pleasing forms everything from the war-paint of the savages to the splendor of temples with all their riches of adornment". So craft-work can be art – but not in art's "highest vocation". In its freedom alone, Hegel writes, "is fine art truly art". Would the highest vocation of craft be a transform of philosophy or religion, as Hegel insists art in its highest vocation has achieved?

Hegel went on to say that art "no longer affords that satisfaction of spiritual needs which earlier ages and nations sought in it". This would have been difficult for the Abstract Expressionists to accept, as they felt themselves to have begun something which Mark Rothko predicted would last a thousand years. And they certainly regarded themselves as concerned with art "in its highest vocation", whether they read Hegel or not: they characterized their work in the most exalted terms available, which meant in the language of philosophy or religion. Most of them, moreover, had lived through a period in which art had been enlisted in various political causes and the declaration of art as free would have expressed the attitude that art should be without ulterior purpose and made solely for its own sake. This remains a tenet of conservative art criticism today: if it is political, it is not art. But even contemporary artists one does not spontaneously regard as conservative have retained the same attitude: the sculptor Richard Serra declared that "As soon as art is forced or persuaded to serve alien values, it ceases to serve its own needs". And further, "To deprive art of its uselessness is to make it other than art".

This might seem to rule out as art all craft products predicated on a notion of function or utility, which become, by Serra's criterion, "other than art". It is conceptually ingenuous to suppose, on the other hand, that craft might automatically achieve the coveted status of art merely by disavowing use – by knocking the spout off the tea-pot, for example and declaring the residue sculpture. I have seen plates by Peter Voulkos with holes, which make them useless for holding soup; or vessels by Ron Nagel with walls too thick and interiors too thin to contain anything much; or cups by Kenneth Price with no bottoms. These are exercises in conceptual mischief. The real problem is to show how craft can be art, whether it is useful or not – and solving this has been among the main efforts of American ceramists since the 1950s.

By a fortunate accident of art history, ceramics happened to be in an advantageous position to challenge the art-craft distinction. Indeed, that distinction may have been a blessing in disguise, for it forced American ceramists to seek ways of blurring if not entirely erasing it, not by forsaking use so much as by finding ways of incorporating artistic discoveries into contemporary ceramic practice, hence of practicing craft and making art at the same time. Lacking the goad of a disenfranchising distinction lent an impetus to the history of ceramics in the United States and accounts for its challenging character. An analogy may be found in recent American politics, where the aim has been to overcome certain traditional divisions, felt to be repressive, between genders or races. This typically involves what the women's movement has called "consciousness raising", which consists in bringing the condition of women to conscious awareness. The recent history of American ceramics has been a form of collective consciousness raising, which would not have happened had not the distance between it and art come to seem intolerable to some. So the idea of a boundary has been a remarkable stimulus to creativity which, since it involves self-definition, inevitably has a philosophical dimension, moving craft near if not under the sphere of "Absolute Spirit", if that concept retains any plausibility.

There is another aspect to ceramic's evolution, however. American art passed through a remarkable number of dramatic internal transformations beginning with the Abstract Expressionists and this has meant that American ceramics itself passed through a number of parallel transformations, once the possibility occurred to ceramists that gesturally handled paint had a natural analogy to gesturally handled clay. Peter Voulkos, the first to seize upon this possibility, formed many of his main ideas in discussion with the artists he encountered at Black Mountain College or in the Cedar Bar in New York, where he absorbed the values and attitudes of Franz Kline, De Kooning and others; and it would have seemed entirely arbitrary to think of Voulkos's work as craft merely because clay was its medium. Indeed, the content of Voulkos's extraordinarily powerful work might be said to be a critique of pure clay – a demonstration of clay's essential properties, much in the way in which De Kooning, whatever he painted, was creating a critique of pure painting. Inevitably, Voulkos appropriated a number of attitudes which belonged to Abstract Expressionism, most especially its primitivism. "Creative art has a better chance of developing from coarseness and courage", he said, "than from culture". [p.79] But to the degree that his work embodies "coarseness", it is as part of its meaning, which implies that primitiveness versus culture is what his ceramics at times is about. In this way, Abstract Expressionist ceramics, as it was inevitably designated, conformed, as we shall see, to the most influential theory of modernist art available.

Voulkos's achievement, it must be emphasized, was facilitated by the fact that he worked with clay, which in its response to touch is as immediate as paint. It would be very difficult to imagine Abstract Expressionist furniture or glass, or metalwork (though Eva Hesse's Metronomic Irregularity II was misdescribed as Pollock in three dimensions). The similarities between the plasticities of paint and clay is what made ceramics the avant-garde craft and indeed enabled it to adapt to its own medium forms of expression which appeared in the internal history of painting. But very quickly, in terms of this history, art went past Abstract Expression. Voulkos was really the only Abstract Expressionist ceramist of importance, though "Abstract Expressionist Ceramics" was the title of an important exhibition at the University of California at Irvine in 1966. Even Voulkos's students, who had internalized so many of his attitudes and emulated his styles of shaping clay, very quickly moved into a style of ceramics closer to what they perceived as happening in movements such as Pop. So once again, ceramics modeled itself and defined its role with reference to what was happening in art. The transition from Voulkos to those who came next in the history was not an internal development in the philosophy of clay so much as the reflection, in the medium of clay-work, of revolutions taking place in advanced visual art. It is this intertwining of two histories which makes the history of ceramics itself too complex to be treated in a linear way, as a succession of stylistic shifts from one episode to another. It is as if the history of art and the history of ceramics were a kind of double helix, with various pairings which themselves may very well have reflected changes in American civilization itself.

Consider, for example, the profound difference in spirit between Voulkos's work and that of Robert Arneson. Voulkos incarnated the artistic idealism of the 1950s and the overall sense of participating in a fresh beginning for American art – a paradigm shift, to borrow from Thomas Kuhn's revolutionary theory of the history of science. The sense of having entered unexplored aesthetic territory might be said to parallel the feeling expressed in the tremendous ambition to explore outer space, to place a man on the Moon – "One small step for man, one large step for Mankind", as Neil Armstrong phrased it. The artist and the astronaut were two vehicles of the same optimism. Small wonder that artists thought of themselves as exalted beings. And small wonder as well that in whatever medium – clay or paint – the work of that era displayed such energy and elan. The world was limitless and the future brilliant if arduous in the vision conveyed by John F. Kennedy in his Inaugural Address of 1961. When Kennedy was assassinated in 1963, this vision had begun to sour. A terribly unpopular war was under way, science was held accountable for its complicity in the war – and as science became suspect, the universities, which sheltered and supported scientific research, themselves became suspect. Artists turned their backs on the heroic sublime and its emblem in physical beauty and found ways to hold mirrors up to American society in which it could see its moral ugliness reflected. By showing itself to itself, the country could see, as with Dorian Gray, a very different look than what it had believed it showed.

It would be difficult to find a more precise expression for this mocking and denunciatory attitude than Arneson's American Standard of 1963, consisting of three aggressively loose effigies of American standard toilets in red, white and blue – the colors of the American flag. It conveyed a violently counter-patriotic metaphor, associating the flag with shit. Duchamp once defended R. Mutt's Fountain – American Standard's art-historical predecessor – by saying that America's chief contribution to civilization was modern plumbing. Arneson, through the use of patriotic colors, identified America with the universal symbol of disgust and executed through American Standard a sullen portrait of the national spirit. America had badly fallen in the esteem of its children. It was no longer "the land of the free and the home of the brave". It was, to use the derisive teutonification of its name adopted by the anti-war protesters, Amerika.

There is no internal history for American ceramics capable of explaining how work like Arneson's should have evolved out of work like Voulkos's – any more than one could see Warhol or Oldenberg as a logical progression beyond Pollock or De Kooning. It is true that the handling of the clay in American Standard retains some of the plastic vitality that Voulkos made central to his work. But it is difficult to imagine Voulkos inscribing words in his pieces, the way Arneson does in the base of American Standard. The glazing seems slap-dash and hurried, as if it were enough that the red, white and blue colors should be legible without being beautiful – America itself had sullied the national colors. And finally, American Standard has something of the scale and raw humor of an item to be found in joke stores and souvenir shops, whose piss-aesthetic was monumentalized twenty years later in the scary fabrications of Jeff Koons, who has no place in the history of ceramics, even if his confections were, in fact, glazed porcelain effigies of Michael Jackson and others. By the time Arneson held his epochal show at Sonnabend, paint had lost a great deal of its Abstract Expressionist mystique and clay had become available for art in so natural a way that it could not be appealed to as a basis for drawing a boundary between ceramics and art. If that boundary still existed, it perhaps had to do with the irrelevance of the artist's hand to high art, where works were increasingly sent out for fabrication and produced in quantity. Since the clay artists, Arneson included, accepted hand-madeness as somehow central to their endeavor, they remained craftspersons, whatever their ulterior ambitions. When Voulkos remarked that there is plenty of craft in art-making, it was perhaps unimaginable to him that painters would abandon the hand, which was after all so central in Abstract Expressionist mythology. It is, on the other hand, difficult to imagine that craftspersons could allow their work to be realized by others, as happens with some frequency with sculptors: how could they continue to think of themselves as craftspersons if the work did not take shape through their touch?

There is a further difference between Voulkos and Arneson as embodiments of two sharply distinct phases of American art history which, as I see it, reflect a sharp change in direction of American moral self-consciousness. I shall endeavor to bring this out by placing their work in a perspective made available through the influential theories of Clement Greenberg. His epochal essay, "Modernist Painting", appeared in 1960 – a crucial date, considering the profound differences between the 1950s and the 1960s. Greenberg characterized Modernism in general and modernism in art in particular, in terms of self-critique, a questioning of its own

foundations. In effect this meant that art became its own subject, seeking to discover "through its own operations and works, the effects exclusive to itself". The model for this, he thought, was in the critical philosophy of Kant: reason, as an exercise of its reflective powers, took itself for its subject and undertook to define its internal limits. For reasons he never attempted to explain historically, Greenberg associated self-critique in art with the identification of "all that was unique in the nature of its medium": each art is obliged, under Modernism, to "eliminate... any and every effect that might conceivably be borrowed from or by the medium of any other art". Through self-criticism, each of the arts would be "rendered pure" of features which belonged essentially to some other art. In the case of painting, for example, Greenberg felt that Modernism led its adherents to the discovery that the essence of painting lay in its flatness: "The stressing of the ineluctable flatness of the surface remained ... more fundamental than anything else to the processes by which pictorial art criticized and defined itself under Modernism". While this did not exclude representation from painting, it did exclude illusion, which requires the use of three-dimensional space, which he believed was essential to sculpture.

Greenberg did not carry his analyses much further than this, but it was perfectly plain that a Modernism of ceramics would be a self-aware search for the essential features of the medium of clay and the exclusion from "pure" ceramics of whatever belonged to some other medium. If three-dimensionality was essential to sculpture and ineliminable from ceramics, for example, ceramics would be annexed to sculpture, unless some other basis for differentiation could be found.

In terms of Greenberg's effort to build a form of art criticism into the identity of Modernist art, Voulkos may be viewed as engaged in a sustained inquiry into the essence of the ceramic medium. He reflected the attitude of the painting culture in which he arrived at his particular vision by making clay and its properties the subject of his art in much the same way in which painting had taken the act of painting as its essential attribute (very few painters took Greenberg's exaltation of flatness seriously). The Abstract Expressionists lived in a world of paint in a way in which Voulkos lived in a world of clay. The ceramist Steven De Staebler told me that there were literally tons of clay in Voulkos's studio at Berkeley. He was, as Walter Hopps remarks, "the first major artist in America to understand how the malleability of clay could fit the

Abstract Expressionist mode". But he also appeared to be following Greenberg's imperative of purity by expunging, at least symbolically, whatever did not belong to ceramic's essence. He was, for example, uncertain of the relevance to ceramics of the idea of the vessel. And I think he was equally uncertain of the relevance to it of color. Hopps speaks of the "dominant use of natural earth tones with few applied colors (blues, blacks and reds)". It was as though the range of colors aesthetically acceptable were those inherent to fired clay.

It is possible to understand other great ceramists as accepting the Greenberghian agenda. Rudi Steffel's Light Gatherers can, by those criteria, be considered a critique of pure porcelain. Steffel's work is about clay and light, while Voulkos's is about clay as matter and darkness. Both exemplify the spirit of self-reference through which Greenberg sought to characterize modernist art. But the essentialist premises of Modernist art, according to Greenberg's theory, were sharply contested in the Sixties and especially the Seventies, when essentialism came under a political and in some ways a philosophical attack. Arneson's work falls squarely in the new era which I sometimes like to think of as the Age of Deconstruction – a term introduced in Jacques Derrida's writings of the late 1960s. There is no settled definition of what the term means, but it conveys the sense of conceptual dismantling which marked the 1960s, especially in America, when America itself was, so to speak, artistically deconstructed and found wanting. The Sixties had to deal with misplaced essentialisms in politics: 1964 was the "Summer of Freedom", during which massive efforts were made to realize the civil rights of Southern Blacks. 1968 saw the beginning of Radical Feminism, in which women undertook to gain for themselves some of the privileges allotted by tradition to males. It is in this context that the animus against essentialism has to be understood. To be an essentialist, in thinking about gender, was to imagine that there is, for example, an essence of womanhood and that certain behaviors and attitudes were essential to being a woman. The counterclaim, frequently enough voiced, was that womanhood is nothing but a social role thrust on women because of biological circumstances, but that any woman could be anything she wanted, without fear of betraying her essence – because there were no such essential feminine features. The question "What is it to be a real woman?" was a Modernist question, encouraging a critique of pure womanhood. So women naturally set about discarding the attributes of femininity, as emblematized in the ritual bra-burnings

of the late Sixties. There might, of course, be a feminine essence. But it need not coincide with the activities to which social practice confined women – the straitened household world with its discontents, frustrations and inhibitions. It would be an essence compatible with alternative sexualities and no limit whatever on what women could become. And precisely this spirit is expressed in Arenson's art. One could no longer legitimately criticize a work as untrue to its essence. Anyone could do anything and by the 1970s, anything could be a work of art. Rose Slivka, writing about the group around Voulkos, says that "There was nothing they were not willing to try". But Arneson demonstrated how narrow were the boundaries of Abstract Expressionist exploration: his work was provocatively impure. Under Deconstructionist attitudes, there were no internal limits on what materials an artist could use. So clay was enfranchised for art by default.

The Abstract Expressionist movement did not long survive the publication of Greenberg's essay and even Greenberg admitted that it was dead as early as 1962 – not that he ever accepted the Deconstructionist aesthetic of the later 1960s. It is consistent with his attitude that movement declined by abandonment of its essential character – by introducing the figure, for example – and that it ought to give way to painting which remained loyal to Modernist imperatives, such as (as he saw it) Color Field Painting. But by the mid-1960s an entirely new way of thinking about art emerged, with the ideas of Duchamp – whom Greenberg barely mentions in his writing – making purity an irrelevant artistic goal. Duchamp rejected sensuousness as unimportant to art, which he thought of as cerebral and cogitative instead, as if art could be turned directly into philosophy. His most important work was a piece of industrial porcelain, at the very least calling into question the critique of industrial society that figured in Arts and Crafts. Since, however, it was the quality of thought rather than the media of the arts, there was no longer a basis for distinguishing invidiously between ceramics and painting. Duchamp disparaged painters who were "in love with the smell of paint". And he would have thought no differently of ceramists in love with the smell of clay. Duchamp's effort as an artistic thinker was to expel tastefulness from the concept of art. His ready-mades were intended to separate art from aesthetics and especially from sensuous beauty, so basic to Greenberg's philosophy of criticism. Whatever the connection between Duchamp and Arneson, the latter was raucously anti-aesthetic – as in the large John with Art of 1964, in the bowl of which the artist modeled some unmistakable turds (=art, in

Arneson's vulgar lexicon). He was a Deconstructivist avant la let-tre, especially in his deconstruction of the Artist in his series of remarkably wry and humorous self-portraits as a grizzled non-hero with sexual obsessions and comical proclivities – sticking his tongue out, being hit by a brick, or shown with his penis exposed as in a Grecian herm. He was an exponent of funk, a term appro-priated from a kind of down and dirty jazz music which exploited howling or growling noises and a heavy beat to express opposition to the ideals of beauty associated with music: funk was true to its etymological origins, as meaning a stench or strong smell. And it spread to modes of dance, costume, speech, behavior, as well as art, which flaunted in its name a willed vulgarity and a broad joki-ness (the humor it exploited set it apart from the later "grunge".) It used whatever material was at hand in whatever way the artist chose, however awkward, tasteless and – well – funky. So it is consistent with the spirit of funk that an artist should use clay in an awkward, tasteless, vulgar and funky way, erasing the bound-aries of Modernism by disregarding them. Purity of medium meant nothing to Arneson and, in his genially anarchic way, he cleared the concept of ceramics of various qualities associated with "the well wrought urn": tastefulness, clarity, perfection and beauty.

If Modernism in principle weakened the distinction between art and craft, Deconstruction erased it almost completely. The medi-um-defining rules were discarded. Why depend upon glazing to impart color to one's pieces? Why not simply paint them with coat upon coat of enamel, as in the work of Ron Nagel or Ken Price? One after another, features which had been believed integral to the concept of ceramics were transformed into options which had no place in the definition of the ceramic art. This applied with special force to the concept of the vessel, with which ceramics was traditionally closely identified and I want to concentrate on the vessel in the remaining pages of this essay.

It followed from Greenberg's essentialist analysis that representa-tion was an accidental feature of painting. So there was no critical imperative to paint the figure and an example of pure painting would seem of necessity to be abstract. This tended to put consid-erable pressure on painters of the figure, who were regarded as betrayers of the future. The vessel in ceramics was the counter-part of the figure in painting. So eliminating the vessel was analo-gous to eliminating the figure from painting, which entailed that pure ceramics should be, as it were, abstract, that is, free of ves-sel. In the liberationist spirit of the Sixties, vesseldom was vassal-

dom and the pot became an emblem of political backwardness. But given the poverty of artistic categorization, there seemed noth-ing for a piece of de-vesselized ceramic to be except – sculpture. The difficulty with this, however, was that the de-vesselized ceramics did not really look like sculpture – it simply looked de-vesselized. Clay and glaze were after all enlisted in the production of vessels from the beginning of human civilization and to detach means from end – or to treat means as end – gave an internal negativity to non-pots, an abandonment of tradition which did not quite merit classification as sculpture. So a new aesthetic had to be worked out. It is one thing to shrug off certain characteriza-tions as not belonging to one's essence. It is another to try to find what does belong to it, if essentialism retains it control over thought. But when the entire apparatus of essence and accident is discarded, the entire quest for essences loses its point. In painting that would mean one could be a figurationist or an abstractionist or both. In ceramics it would mean that one could form vessels or not. In feminism, I suppose, a woman could devote herself to her family or take a challenging job, or both. What had looked like imperatives, grounded in one's essential nature, became options, any one of which was consistent with the concept of painting, ceramics, or femininity. Once it was recognized that the concept of ceramics was compatible with an open disjunction of possible realizations, pluralism all at once seemed the only way to think about it. And that is the condition American ceramics is in today.

To discuss the vessel in today's pluralist art world, I must put in place a piece of philosophy that first occurred to me in 1964, when I saw an exhibition of Andy Warhol's Brillo Box sculptures at the Stable Gallery in New York. Brillo Box raised for me the ques-tion of why it was art and how could one tell, since it visually resembled, to any degree one chose, the humble cartons in which Brillo pads were shipped and stored in supermarkets. Of course, if we extend the concept of art to cover commercial art, the utilitari-an container becomes a work of art in its own right. But still it is quite a different work than Brillo Box and it is worth determining how two things, which look entirely alike, can be entirely different. In my view, it has to do with differences in meaning. The com-mercial Brillo Box is designed to celebrate its product: the carton graphically proclaims Brillo's cleanliness and speed in removing grease. Warhol's Brillo Box does not do that. Its artistic content is perhaps commercial reality itself, which it represents through imi-tation. What Warhol celebrated was daily American life, with its Cokes, its hot-dogs, its cans of soup, its detergents – the menu of predictable and satisfying objects which define contemporary life. The philosophical implications of Brillo Box, however, are truly cataclysmic. If works of art and mere things – if works of high and commercial art – can look alike, the looks of things drop entirely out of the concept of visual art, which means that art works can look any way at all. What makes the difference between art and its non-art semblables is not appearance, but meaning. At the same time, aesthetics gives way to interpretation as the appropriate response to art. With this there is no alternative to pluralism as the condition of artistic product.

I have found the existence of indiscernible pairs a powerful stimulant in the philosophy of art and it is clear that it can be applied directly to the vexed problems of ceramics. I once invented an example in which the pottery of two unconnected tribes turned out to look exactly alike – but the pots of Tribe A were ritual objects where the pot of Tribe B were merely pots (in compensation, the baskets of Tribe B were ritual objects where the indiscernible baskets of Tribe A were merely baskets.) It is after all not impossible to imagine a sculpture of a pot which looks exactly like the pot which serves as its model. The difference, again, is in the meaning: the sculpture, at the very least, has the pot as its meaning, the way a quotation has a sentence as its meaning. The meaning of the pot itself is its use, say as storage. That the pot has a use, of course, will not entail that a sculpture of a pot has that use. Sculpture, since art, possesses "aboutness": the sculpture of a pot is about the pot. It might be about the use of the pot, but use and aboutness are different modes of meaning entirely: a pot has a set of uses without possessing aboutness, which belongs altogether to the concept of representation..

Against this kind of example, we can dissolve the question of the relationship between art and craft. The hand-made pottery alluded to in my first paragraph has the use that pots and dishes have as standard – usually the same uses their mass-produced counterparts have. It is their made-by-handedness – their non-standardness – which qualified their makers as critics of Industrial society. They are artifacts. They are artifacts even if decorated and embellished. As we learn from Robert Venturi, decorating a shed does not transform it into a piece of architecture. To believe that it does is to commit what I think of as The Aesthetic Fallacy. But for each such artifact, a work of ceramic art can be imagined which looks exactly like it. The artwork will differ from its artifactual counterpart through its meaning, which has to be brought to awareness through interpretation.

This, I believe, gives us some purchase on those artists in the present exhibition who have persisted in the face of considerable opposition to use the vessel: William Daley, Rudi Steffel, Adrian Saxe and Betty Woodman, to name but some. For them, vessel is content: it is what their work is about. I once wrote as follows about Woodman: As a craftsperson, she makes vases as her most salient product; as an artist, she takes the vase as her most salient subject. So the vase, in her oeuvre, exists on two planes at once and answers to two sets of imperatives. And this is true of the other vessel-makers I have mentioned. One could stick flowers in Steffel's vases, pour wine into Saxe's Baroque urns, fill Daley's Danced Place dish with peanuts. But as art their works have entirely different kinds of meanings: metaphysical, historical, ritualistic. Woodman's vases acknowledge her empathy with countless artisans in perhaps every civilization who, from before the dawn of industrial manufacture, produced vessels for the various necessary uses vessels serve and who have mastered the primordial technologies of firing and glazing objects of clay. But they also acknowledge in their brilliant glazing the women who filled, carried and emptied them: it is as if her vases are metaphors for their female users. Her work brings to self-consciousness the uses ceramic products have played in different forms of life throughout history. By contrast, Adrian Saxe's flamboyant pots celebrate the great Baroque porcelains, looking, as they do, like trophies or extravagant gifts, to be given by one German princeling to another. So his works refer to a particular moment in the history of ceramics and celebrate the extravagance, the opulence and the aesthetic foolishness of Dresden ware. Steffel exploits the translucence of porcelain, using his vessels to unite the human with the cosmic – the Let-there-be-light of Genesis. Daley's Dancing Place, one feels, makes reference to bowls in which water or milk or grain might be placed for the ritual purposes dances serve in enlisting the help of the gods. Wherever it is set, that becomes a dancing place and a place of sacrifice. These works, for all that they involve the vessel, are examples of free art, though the vessels themselves are dependent. Part of the meaning of the works are the modes of interaction between human beings and vessels, which touch on "the deepest interests of mankind and the most comprehensive truths of the spirit".

Even when they are in a sense vessels, the works I have been describing have meanings associated with vessels as these figure in different forms of life. But it is consistent with ceramic art that it can have other meanings than those associated with vessels. With Kenneth Price and James Melchert, for example, we find exploration of forms which in some way celebrate ceramics itself – in scale or surface or color – rather than the traditional uses of ceramic objects. Melchert's Big A sculpture, big for an A but not big for a sculpture, expresses the possibilities of meaning open to ceramics and calls for a very different form of interpretation than works which are about the traditional uses of fired clay. Price's work has an astonishing delicacy, a monument as it were to clay's fragility. Ron Nagel creates portraits of imaginary cups, preserving the lightness of these little containers in which we imbibe stimulants like tea or coffee, inviting us to feel that lightness bodily, the way we feel the lightness of the finest china and providing a stimulant for poetic thought as we turn one of his cups over in our hands, mark the surface and the way it refracts light and attend to the implications of their forms.

I have only sought to illustrate the kinds of interpretation that belong by rights to ceramic objects which are works of art. Parallel interpretations will occur to viewers in connection with each of the works in this exhibition, and with a great many works not included here. It is fitting that ceramic art should have attained self-consciousness as we approach the new millennium, leaving behind conceptions of itself which derive from the kind of bias expressed in judgment by Peter Schjeldahl that "You cannot make high art from the potter's craft". You can. You just have to recognize that the "potter's craft" yields objects which can become high art when infused with the structures of meaning which interpretation recovers for us. I also feel that it is fitting that this recognition should have occurred in American ceramics, which has had so epic a history in the past decades and which has so arduous a path to follow in the search for its identity as art.

THE PERSISTENCE OF VESSELS

by Janet Koplos

The 40-year period represented by this selection of American ceramic works from the collection of Museum Het Kruithuis was a time of growth and change and excitement. Many of the most celebrated names of the period are included in this group of works, which could be described as an all-star line-up, with one or two quirks – and that's appropriate, for quirks are a regular feature, a desired option, in the pluralist history of American clay.

This selection can also be regarded as a study of the importance of the vessel in contemporary American ceramics, illustrating how the formal qualities of vessels contribute to even sculptural or pictorial works. The vessel, most often wheel-thrown, coiled or cast, has been a basic ceramic form throughout the whole of human history ('vessel' is a generalising term currently used to identify the familiar container form of pottery without linking it to the functional aspect associated with the word 'pot'). Clay may also be modelled, as in figurines, or a form can be constructed from slabs. To some extent clay can be handled and shaped as sculptural bulk, but its need to dry evenly and to pass through the high heat of the kiln in order to become resistant to breakage sets lim-

its to its solid massing. Thus clay is best shaped into a wall or membrane of relatively consistent thickness. One wall can support another by intersecting or a single wall can be free-standing if it is a circular continuity – i.e. a cylinder. A cylinder when closed at one end makes a vessel. There you have it.

In addition to these technical reasons, the vessel remains a primary ceramic form because the multiple roles it has played in human life still suit contemporary purposes and preferences. The vessel was central to religious rituals and social ceremonies. It has always been available both to be used and to be looked at. It told stories, bore symbols, conveyed status, carried meaning. It has never been limited in style, nor particularly limited in scale: it can be thimble-size or big enough for several people to climb into. The form can be open or closed. As an object, the vessel can refer to or imitate another thing from the real world, or it can exist as an unquantifiable abstraction. The vessel wall can be sculpturally manipulated or it can be addressed two-dimensionally, as a 'canvas' for pictures or decorations that happens to cut through space three-dimensionally. In addition, the surface can be an arena for an assortment of tactile experiences. This world of capabilities is so broad that the vessel format is almost never a curb on an artist's imagination or a liability to significant expression.

The works in this selection date from the late fifties to the mid-nineties (with the exception of the works of George Ohr). They are concentrated in two temporal clumps – the sixties and the eighties. Because the artists included worked across the post-war time span, the grouping gives a sense of the sweep of issues across those years. Still, the works do not make a perfect chronology, and it's more useful to approach them with the idea of studying the specific instances that these exemplary artists represent: here you see what some of the best people in the field have discovered, and the matters that have engaged them in this particular artistic medium. The focus of the collection and this publication is the art quality of the works.

The one artist included who is outside the post-war time span is George Ohr, a potter active in the American South around the turn of the century. He was an anomaly then, a 'character' whose work was little known and soon forgotten. But a huge cache of his pottery was rediscovered in 1972 and met with great acclaim, being acquired by noted artists and art collectors as well as ceramic aficionados. Ohr worked almost exclusively with vessels, but he

Fig. 1
Peter Voulkos
Gallas Rock, 1959-61
sculpture, 244 cm
collection of Frederick S. Wight Art
Galleries, University of California,
Los Angeles.

pushed them beyond usefulness into eccentric, delicate and suggestive forms. Exaggeration, such as the elaborate handles on one of the pots shown here, is an Ohr characteristic, and he also typically worked with extremely thin edges that ripple like a wilting flower petal, or with thin walls which he twisted, making his vessels look on the verge of collapse. This baroque decadence – mixing technical skill, decorative elaboration and implications of decay or destruction – along with Ohr's assertive self-identification as an art potter making one-of-a-kind works, struck a chord in the late 20th century ceramic world and has been influential.

The deformation of Ohr's vessels was well received in the 1970s because the way had been prepared by the rather more coarse and aggressive deformation of Peter Voulkos and his students of the late fifties and early sixties. Voulkos was a pioneer of the sculptural strategy of closing and stacking vessels. Closing – minimising the importance of the interior by shrinking the pot's mouth – was an attempt to eliminate 'receptacle' considerations and associations so the work could more easily be understood as a sculptural form (although, since it remained a hollow volume, it was still essentially a pot). Stacking – accumulating mass in a precariously balanced and roughly tactile configuration – created feelings of dynamism and risk (fig. 1).

Many other artists also closed the vessel, although often in a more careful and restrained manner. For example, Malcolm McClain's Chamber of Spheres (1956-57) (fig. 2) is constructed of multiple independent hollow volumes – that is, vessels – that have been stacked in a tree-like configuration. McClain shows no interest in painterly surface but keeps to a neutral and continuous tone that encourages focus on form. The pale colour and elevated mass give a sense of lightness that makes this sculpture evoke a cloud, but this cloud, in the Cold War era, must have elicited the ominous association of an atomic bomb. Another significant employer of vessel closure is Toshiko Takaezu, whose many large pieces retain only a vestigial mouth or merely an air hole that allows air to escape during firing of the piece. Takaezu started by closing small works but has also made them as tall as a person, treating them as canvases for abstract glaze effects that relate both to ceramic precedents and to abstract colour fields in painting of the 1950s, when she began working (fig. 3).

Three early-sixties vessels by Voulkos in this Kruithuis selection might be described as mid-career works. He began, as Picasso

Fig. 2
Malcolm McClain
Chamber of Spheres, 1956-57
65 x 48 x 49 cm
Colletion Museum Het Kruithuis

Fig. 3
Toshiko Takaezu
Burst II, 1993-97
147 x 76 cm
courtesy Charles Cowles Gallery,
New York

Fig. 4
John Mason
Vertical Sculpture, 1962
162,5 x 40,6 x 30,5 cm

private collection

did, by learning all the rules and making excellent conventional works; in clay that means vases, tureens and the like. Voulkos then worked at forgetting the rules. Influenced by Abstract Expressionist painting in the 1950s, he made large, vertical ceramic sculptures in which gesture was shown in the receptive surface and immediacy was conveyed by the rough stacking and joining of the parts. His early students/peers also worked in this manner, notably John Mason, who created free-standing sculptures with powerfully dynamic forms and surfaces, as well as massive panels of gesturally agitated clay in monumental walls (fig. 4).

Voulkos's looseness was also realised in less complex unitary forms, such as the bowls and vase shown here. His exploration naturally led to the use of non-traditional materials, such epoxy paint instead of glazes. His square bowl and vase here are related: both are oversize, both have a chunky angularity, and both are given a similar division of colour and space (a stripe of black, a short stroke on a terracotta expanse). These works, and also his unpainted low bowl with the dramatically split rim, have a striking physical presence, an aura that communicates itself to an attentive viewer. Part of the power comes from the irregularity of the forms and the roughness of their profiles. There is no gloss, no smooth visual surge of the sort expected in traditional 'nice' ceramic bowls and vases. Rather, these works affect the eyes of viewers like sandpaper, communicating sensation so that it seems that one's eyes are extensions of one's skin. With these works, Voulkos reduces his fully sculptural play – which he had recently begun to express in bronze, a material that allowed drastic extensions of line that clay did not – to concentrate on a constructive sense of form and a heightened surface interest. He also addressed surface character in gestural, tactile relief paintings. In recent decades Voulkos has dealt with increasingly subtle colour but equally physical alterations of surface form in thick plates and other manipulated forms such as 'ice buckets' (fig. 5).

James Melchert, a student/peer of Voulkos's at Berkeley, started with ragged forms and non-traditional surfaces such as the 'Small Silver Cup' here, which is like a metal flask, without the refinement of traditional ceramics. The 'First Ghost Box' also shows Melchert's inquisitiveness and provocativeness in its sloppy form, slapdash colour and unknown something oozing out of the top. Among Melchert's important innovations in the ceramics field is a pot with a horizontal orientation (fig. 6) that, by being atypical, called attention to its sculptural aspects. The 'Zipper Pouch' in the Kruithuis selection has the same impact: it does not match any established ceramic configuration, so one must explore it visually and give language to its effects. It appears to be two lengths of a collapsed tube, folded, pushed together, and coated with a frosting-like patch of white. The elements are utterly simple and the work would seem to be purely formal, defined by the making process. However, associations persist. The loops in the tubes make a rudimentary container, reminding us of clay's history of service, and together the two linear elements look like figures under a blanket.

Another Melchert contribution to ceramics is his conceptual orientation. Not only has he made performance pieces (the best known – several men dipping their heads in buckets of clay slip and waiting for it to dry in an unevenly heated room – was staged in Amsterdam in 1972), a large series of works on the subject of the letter 'a' also give vent to his playful intelligence. He made an element of language concrete, while the letter 'a' was a clever choice because each work could punningly be called 'a sculpture.' To use language rather than image was in sympathy with the conceptual practice in the New York art world of the time. To be funny rather than serious was in keeping with the American ceramics world's cutting edge.

The ceramic artist most celebrated for wit and irreverence is Robert Arneson. Compared with Melchert's work, Arneson's is vulgar. The tone is strikingly different: Arneson's humour, particularly in the beginning, is the bad-boy sort, based on 'not-nice' subjects from defecation to nose-picking, with a substantial number of sex references, mostly of the sniggering, locker-room type. The group of works from the sixties in this selection presents a wonderful slice of that time, with Arneson in all his offensive glory. The 'American Standard' sculpture features red, white and blue toilets in a row, 'Breast Trophy' is crowned with two exaggeratedly pointed mounds like a cartoon from an old-style men's magazine and 'Jewel Box,' with its penis handle on the lid, puns on the slang term 'family jewels' (testicles).

Arneson's works arise from the figurine tradition and are pictorial in orientation, although they occupy three-dimensional space. After the sixties, they grew increasingly skilful and refined in details – more lifelike, less cartoonish, less garish – yet the intelligence behind Arneson's humour is consistent throughout his

Fig. 5
Peter Voulkos
Little Nauga, 1983
29 x 34 cm
private collection, Tokyo

Fig. 6
James Melchert
Leg Pot 1, 1962
28 x 81 x 33 cm
collection American Craft Museum,
New York

Fig. 7
Robert Arneson
Classical Exposure, 1972
244 x 91 x 61 cm

collection Daniel Fendrick Family
Washington DC

career. Take, for instance, the title 'American Standard.' That is, in the first place, the name of a commercial brand of plumbing products – which are, of course, made of ceramic. In addition, 'a standard' is another word for a flag, and these plumbing fixtures are the colours of the American flag. Third, 'a standard' can refer to a measure or criteria, so by using the term Arneson calls up the idea of categories, qualities and expectations of art in a very broad sense, and perhaps even asks, in a challenging way, if America is setting the standard for ceramic art. The work is tacky-looking, but its provocations are considerable and impressive.

In this group of works, the 1969 plate includes Arneson's own image. Most of his best-known sculptures feature his face (and sometimes other parts of him as well – fig. 7). With the exception of his Alice Street works, Arneson's use of autobiography is curiously impersonal. It's as if his face is just raw material. Surely he was not motivated by narcissism, because he continually mocks his identity and capabilities in his works, even as he teases the nature of 'self-expression' and the idea that a painted gesture or sculpted form is 'personal' to the artist. Arneson's works always ask questions about the pretensions of his field, his gender, his generation. His later works also address social and political issues – a broader canvas but not necessarily a 'better' one. Still, his sculpture might be contrasted to the equally amusing but shallower work of David Gilhooly, a compatriot in humour in the California Funk movement. Gilhooly is represented here by a 'Hippo Foot Stool,' a thick hassock that plays off the exotic elephant's foot convention. (It seems, though, to be upholstered with the hide of another creature.) Gilhooly is known for often-repulsive depictions of food – the 'Frog and Vegetable Tureen with Human Handle' gives a good idea of such works – and his jokey frog series, including Mao Tse Toad (1976).

Also deriving from the figurine tradition is the large body of work made over the last quarter of a century by Viola Frey, here represented by a figural grouping from 1993. Frey's work is influenced by painting (the figurative painting prominent in the Bay Area in the 1950s), by her collection of flea-market figurines, and by childhood nightmares. She is particularly known for larger-than-life-size individual figures dissolving in a welter of dots of colour, and for figure groups in a variety of sizes. The groups have sometimes suggested eras or stories (e.g., a family of the 1950s). But even when they seem as random as a collection of figurines on a shelf, like the work included here, there is a curious sense of self-consciousness, as if individual figures are aware of their odd positions in this mixture. Frey stirs up questions of personal psychology in such works, which also seem to refer to America's heterogeneity.

Ken Price and Ron Nagle are associated with the early days of hyperstimulation, which centred around Voulkos as a teacher in Los Angeles and the San Francisco Bay Area. They are represented in the Kruithuis collection by works from a 25-year period – 1960 to 1985. Both start with the crudeness that we've already noted in early sixties works by other artists, and proceed to an extremely controlled, almost obsessively perfect surface on small objects. Both can be related to the 'Finish Fetish' style, which grew out of California car culture and its interestingly florid and fussy masculine decoration, which was also realised in sculpture and painting (the perfect gloss on fibreglass sculptures by John McCracken, crisp shapes by Tony DeLap). One more coincidence: both Price and Nagle are represented here by (among other things) an object in a case.

Despite all these commonalities, Price and Nagle are certainly not making the same work. While Price's earliest piece here is a vessel, and his complex installation on the theme of tourist pottery, 'Happy's Curios,' is well known, his practice has been to invent forms more often than to work with standard ceramic shapes. Of his generation, he has been perhaps the most sculpturally inventive (John Mason is the competition), yet he has done so on a diminutive scale – smaller than Joel Shapiro's little sculptures that surprised the art world, and earlier as well. The works included in this publication give a good idea of his range of form – mounds, Constructivist planes, Bauhaus geometrics, and stonelike masses. His recent works (fig. 8) are more roundly (and erotically) organic. They always have openings, but rarely at the top, like a conventional pot. Throughout the development of all these forms, Price has concentrated on surfaces and edges, employing colours that are exquisitely modulated with 'soft' non-glossy and non-metallic finishes. He uses colour to define form and to create atmosphere, simultaneously and inseparably.

Nagle's two oldest works in the group shown here are large and without much colour, precisely the opposite of the remainder of his included works. It's as if the exception proves the rule: he tried out generous, irregular forms that seem patted into shape as well as colours as subtle as those of Japanese pottery, and he

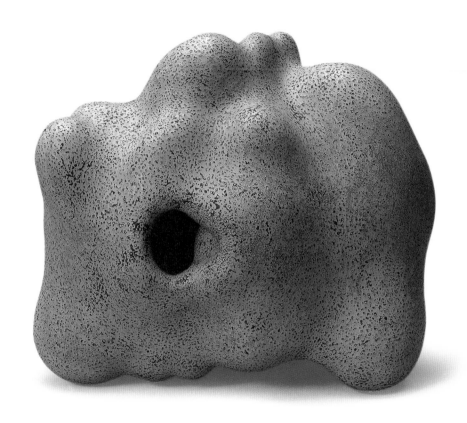

succeeded in producing objects that are quirky, interesting, almost funny. And that was enough of that. His untitled cup from only a year later is recognisably 'a Nagle.' For one thing, it is a cup. The cup form is the Maypole around which he has danced for 30 years. His cups have not been standardised – they have, in fact, steadily atrophied over the years, as the tiny sculptures from the mid-eighties show: we see only a bare mass-with-shard organisation that recalls the once-explicit cup-with-handle form. Some works are thin-walled and some are thick, but all Nagle's forms, as this group of them shows, have a nervous tension combined with a quality of reserve in form and surface. The colours come in a rich variety but are rarely as primary or bright as Price's. Nagle's forms are hard and sharp, almost unnatural, but his various colours speak more often of the earth and its atmosphere: sunsets, rusty stones, fog, limpid waters, mud. This unexpected relationship contributes to the strange energy of the works.

Richard Devore also makes references to nature: he evokes soil – the skin of the earth – as well as human skin. His colours are a huge range of earth tones, which also, as it happens, are skin colours. The surfaces of his pots look dry and cracked, but whether they are meant to be a long view of parched mud flats or a close-up of ageing flesh is impossible to say. The forms unques-

Fig. 8
Ken Price
Hairless, 1997
40 x 47 x 35,5 cm
courtesy Franklin Parrasch Gallery,
New York

21

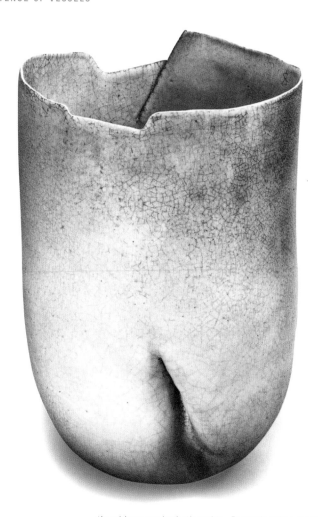

Fig. 9
Richard Devore
untitled, 1980
43 x 30 cm

tionably rouse body thoughts: Devore's taller, narrower vessels, which are not represented in this selection, often have puckers or clefts in the walls, and both those and the low, wide bowls shown here may have interior-bottom orifices or folds reminiscent of intimate anatomy (fig. 9). Yet the works can at the same time be likened to wind-eroded rock or water-worn earthen banks. Over the years, Devore's vessels have been constant in their overall effect, yet remarkably varied in their details, just as human bodies are all the same format yet differ in particulars. He adheres to the vessel configuration, probably for all the reasons already considered and also because a vessel can be placed at hand, and at body level, in a closer relationship to the viewer than that permitted by a large sculpture on a plinth or a painting hanging on a wall.

Somewhat related to the irregular and evocative contours of Devore's vessels are those of Robert Forman, a little-known ceramist who worked in the late seventies and early eighties. The lip contours of his works are particularly striking, especially when the exterior of the vessel is a rich, warm colour with a burnished sheen borrowed from Native American ceramics. Forman's elegant forms are blocky in a faintly anthropomorphic way – as if they represented people with broad shoulders, or someone standing with a hip thrust out. They are more robust and energetic – perhaps 'quicker' – than Devore's sensuous restraint. Robert Turner is

best known for flat-bottomed, sturdy vessels with even more of a sense of sinew and groundedness than Forman's evoke, such as 'Akan V'. Turner's pots are generally thick-walled yet never stodgy because they stay close to the sense of container or enclosure – sometimes suggesting primitive architecture, such as a hut or yurt. Onto these strong, terse, self-contained forms, he may inscribe a single line with the forceful grace and evocativeness of a Zen brushstroke, which is the case in his work called 'Shoreline' that is part of the Kruithuis collection.

William Daley's long career is represented by two examples, vessels whose angularity evokes architecture with breathing room – that is, a man-made landscape. The dish is a relatively modest example of Daley's constructions, which, as the 'Columnar Form' shows, can be expansive in all dimensions. They are more accordion-folded in larger sizes but all works give equal emphasis to inside and outside, so that the vessel wall seems to be a membrane between two equal 'places.' The briefer career of Graham Marks, a generation younger than Daley, is represented by a single piece. His work, like Daley's, consists of complex surfaces constructed in large-scale vessel configurations. But he is known for forms that are organic rather than architectural. They may suggest fantastic seeds or wondrous caves; the fascination of their interior surfaces takes them out of the ordinary, even in comparison with other ceramic vessels.

Rudolf Staffel's 'Light Gatherer' vessels also maintain a sense of inside and outside, not so much as doubleness but as a radiant continuity. In Staffel's translucent porcelain vessels, light passing through the walls almost seems to dissolve them. The works are small but give a powerful and tender sense of the hand, uniting directness and delicacy of touch. Staffel, the oldest of the living artists whose works are shown here, has long worked on shaping light by means of veils of opacity and translucency plus small, intense infusions of colour. His grainy porcelain seems to be composed of solidified light energy. The works of Christina Bertoni, a much younger artist, are quite opposite to Staffel's yet produce a related effect. Her vessels condense patterns on smooth surfaces that seem impossibly far away. The results might appear to be pictures of the cosmos, with the pot surface like a picture plane, the point at which a distant view registers. The consequence is that her bowl forms, which look clear and unequivocal in themselves, visually dissolve under the force of the pattern. Wayne Higby likewise treats the pot surface as a picture plane for a depiction of great spaces, but his works limn the mountain landscapes of the American West – they are terrestrial visions rather than cosmic ones like Bertoni's. Higby's works feature a preferred viewpoint from which the view is perfectly resolved, and he treats the bowl's interior as the middle ground in his perspective expanse.

Surface effects are also a major feature in the work of Betty Woodman. Surprisingly, form is of equal importance, and more surprisingly still, her inventions of form still hold close to pottery standards and remain usable. Woodman, who started working in clay about 50 years ago as a production potter, has gone through numerous evolutions on the way to conceptual yet still functional forms. The 'Letter Holder' in this selection is functional in a magnified, fantastic way. Decoration, which one might expect to be keyed to the rotary plan of vessels and to be comfortingly repetitive, instead grows and spreads and seems to breathe on its own. In Woodman's multipart works in particular, such as the 'Lindos' triptych of vases shown here, line and colour jump from object to object and establish independent rhythms, patterns and spaces. The decoration, especially as it is carried by the eccentric slab handles, is baroque – complex, full, shifting, sensuous. But at the same time, the effect feels contemporary, even post-modern, in its visual mixing and emotional unfetteredness.

As one notes in looking at Woodman's jug and her 'pillow pitchers,' her inflated, exaggerated forms have a visual compulsion of their own, and the works are no less interesting when they are undecorated. The 'pillow pitcher,' one of her most celebrated forms, is easier to read as pneumatic and exuberant in the unglossy, uncolourful example: it looks succinct and resolute. The glazed 'pillow pitcher,' on the other hand, shows why Woodman is sometimes discussed as a painter. The strength of her brushstrokes and her sharp colour contrasts are like underscorings and exclamation marks, while the fluid drips of the glazes and the softer colours are painterly almost to the point of being romantic.

Andrea Gill also makes vases that are intensely decorated, but she operates within the 'frame' provided by the vessel's profile rather than across or between several forms. She tends to work with the faces of a vase rather than its roundedness, just as Woodman does. Her colours and shapes reverberate, one within another. Ron Baron is known for art gallery shows of non-ceramic works. He creates amusing classical vases of stacked objects rescued from attics or garages (briefcases, kitchen equipment, sports paraphernalia), and he has constructed similar forms of shaped ceramic slabs suitable for exhibition outdoors. Baron addresses the notion of ceremonial vessels, such as amphorae and trophies, and no matter what their material his works are simultaneously evocations, representations and intellectualisations. Rhonda Zwillinger is also associated with non-ceramic materials. She was among the artists identified with New York's 'East Village' phenomenon of the early eighties and its aesthetic of excess. She showed installations of garish paintings as textured as cake frosting and amusingly over-embellished pieces of furniture and decorative objects. Following this precedent, her 'Pistol Packing Mama' in the Kruithuis collection suggests a voluptuous, gaudily decorated female, meant for enjoyment.

Adrian Saxe also makes intellectualisations of vases. His works draw on ceramic history, with the added interest of superb craftsmanship. Saxe's high style and virtuoso output suggests a mannerist era following years of great developments and significant art, and they incorporate the humour that is so often present in American ceramics. This humour is not, however, the vulgarity of the sixties or the goofiness of the seventies but a distinctly nineties combination of irony, incongruity and glitter. The finesse of his work certainly has Continental precedents, but may also recall the fancier works of George Ohr. Kathy Butterly's vessels also recall Ohr at times, as filtered perhaps through Arneson and Saxe, and adding both a nod to animated cartoon imagery and a distinctly female sensibility and sensuality. Her tiny pots are raised up on ornate bases or stands. Often, as is the case in this Kruithuis selection, they involve fleshy curves and inward folds such as those associated with the female body. Butterly's forms are typically fluid; 'Splash' specifically represents flow. Her use of simple, intense colouring does not confuse viewers' understanding of form, and perhaps even heightens the eroticism of the works by clinging so tightly to the succulent curves.

No small selection of artists could summarise all the currents in American ceramics. Some categories of work – notably the functional – are missing from this selection. But the liveliness of these varied works, the intensity of form, the emotional tenor of colour, the attention to history, the vigour of contact with the clay substance, the embedded allusions to the body and other specific messages and associations, all propose the complex plurality of American ceramics and demonstrate its artistic quality. ●

Robert Arneson

Ronald Baron

Christina Bertoni

Kathy Butterly

William Daley

Richard Devore

Robert Forman

Viola Frey

David Gilhooly

Andrea Gill

Wayne Higby

Graham Marks

James Melchert

Ron Nagle

George Ohr

Ken Price

Adrian Saxe

Rudolf Staffel

Robert Turner

Peter Voulkos

Betty Woodman

Rhonda Zwillinger

American Standard   *sculpture, 1965   9,5 x 20,5 x 18 cm*

Zig Spout Tea Pot *teapot, 1969   25 x 29,5 x 17 cm*

Robert Arneson

Foot Finger Box   *sculpture, 1965   17,5 x 24,5 x 19,5 cm*

Breast Trophy *sculpture, 1964   47,5 x 24,5 x 20,5 cm*

Robert Arneson

Jewel Box *box with cover, 1964   20 x 12,5 x 12 cm*

untitled *teapot, 1969   28 x 29 x 16,5 cm*

untitled (Alice Street Series) *plate, 1967 44,5 cm*

History of the US II (Stack XXVI) *vase form, 1992   75 x 27 cm*

Making ends meet (Stack XXV) *vase form, 1992   75 x 40 cm*

Flat Circuits   multipartite sculpture, ca. 1980   *9 x 31 cm*

untitled bowl, 1980 *12,5 x 23,5 cm*

Christina Bertoni

New Fuse   bowl, ca. 1980   *11 x 22 cm*

What does this mean? dish, 1984   *6,8 x 33 x 21,5 cm*

Kathy Butterly

Tip Toe cup, 1998 *12 x 6 cm*

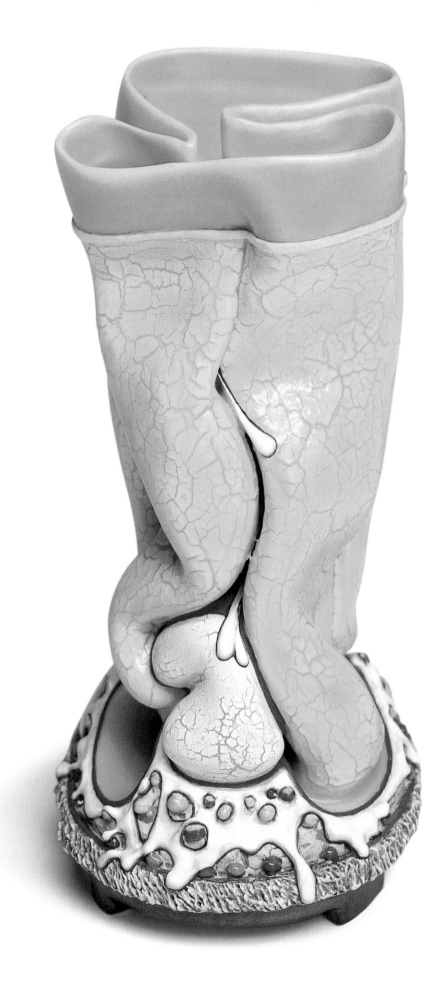

Splash   cup, 1998   *12,3 x 6,5 x 5,8 cm*

Royal Float cup, 1998 *13 x 8 x 4,5 cm*

William Daley

Danced place   sculpture, 1982   *32 x 64 x 64 cm*

Columnar Form sculpture, 1978 *103 x 48 x 48 cm*

untitled   bowl, ca. 1977   *13,3 x 28 cm*

untitled bowl, 1980 *9 x 17,8 cm*

untitled bowl, 1980 *7 x 24,3 cm*

untitled   pot, 1981   *18 x 23,5 cm*

untitled pot, 1981 *18 x 23,5 cm*

untitled pot, 1981 *20 x 21,5 cm*

Viola Frey

Artist Mind Artist Studio   sculpture, 1993   *146 x 175 x 70 cm*

Hippo Foot Stool sculpture, 1965 *44 x 35 x 32 cm*

Frog Tostada sculpture, 1980 *8 x 13,8 cm*

Frogsicle sculpture, 1980 *5,8 x 17,5 x 8,5 cm*

David Gilhooly

Television's Revenge of Frog Elvis   sculpture, ca. 1978   *45 x 32 x 30 cm*

Camel atop Vegetables   sculpture, ca. 1978   *60 x 43 x 44 cm*

Frog and Vegetable Tureen with Human Handle   sculpture, 1975   *28 x 28,5 x 28,5 cm*

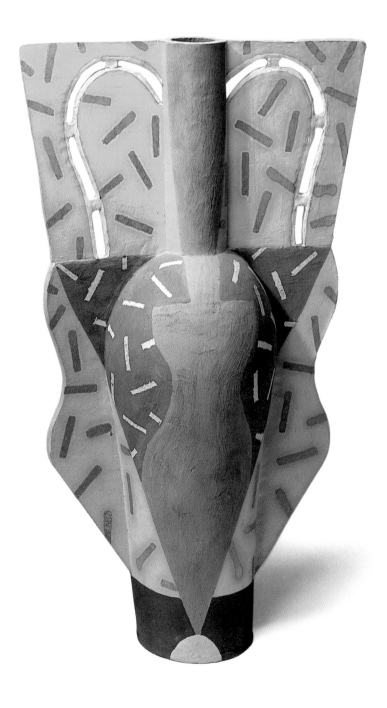

Painted Amphora   vase, 1980   66,5 x 40,5 x 20,5 cm

untitled vase, 1982 70,5 x 46 x 15 cm

Rim Lake: Maurice's View   bowl, 1982   *28,5 x 48,5 x 43 cm*

South Park bowl, 1977 *32,5 x 56,7 x 34 cm*

untitled   sculpture, ca. 1980-1982   *73 x 75 x 72 cm*

First Ghost Box box with cover, ca. 1964 *18 x 20 x 15 cm*

Zipper Pouch   sculpture, ca. 1966   *6,8 x 21 x 11,2 cm*

James Melchert

Small Silver Cup   vase, 1958   *9,5 x 9,5 x 9,5 cm*

Hand With Ashtray   sculpture, ca. 1970   *17 x 41,5 x 41 cm*

Big A   sculpture, 1969   *51,5 x 48,5 x 23,8 cm*

untitled   pot with lid, ca. 1960   *25 x 22,8 x 14,2 cm*

Blue Bread Jar with Heart   pot with lid, ca. 1960   *25 x 53,5 x 22 cm*

Ron Nagle

untitled   cup, 1969   *7,5 x 11 x 9 cm*

untitled cup, 1967 *7,6 x 8 x 7,5 cm*

untitled cup, 1961 *11,5 x 7,8 x 6 cm*

Ron Nagle

untitled   cup, ca. 1969   *9 x 12,7 x 8,3 cm*

untitled   cup, 1975   *10 x 11 x 8 cm*

Ron Nagle

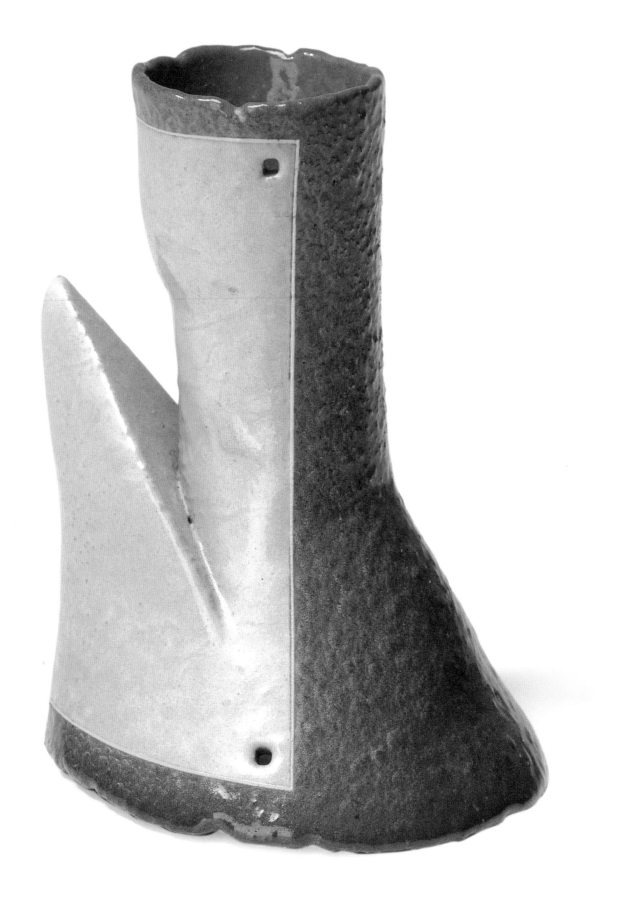

untitled sculpture, 1983 *8 x 6,5 cm*

untitled sculpture, 1984 *10 x 7,5 x 5,5 cm*

Decoyama # 1 sculpture, 1978 *9,7 x 9,7 x 8,3 cm*

Sighter cup, 1995 *11 x 8,5 x 7 cm*

Bird/Twig Cup cup, 1992 *7,5 x 6 x 4,8 cm*

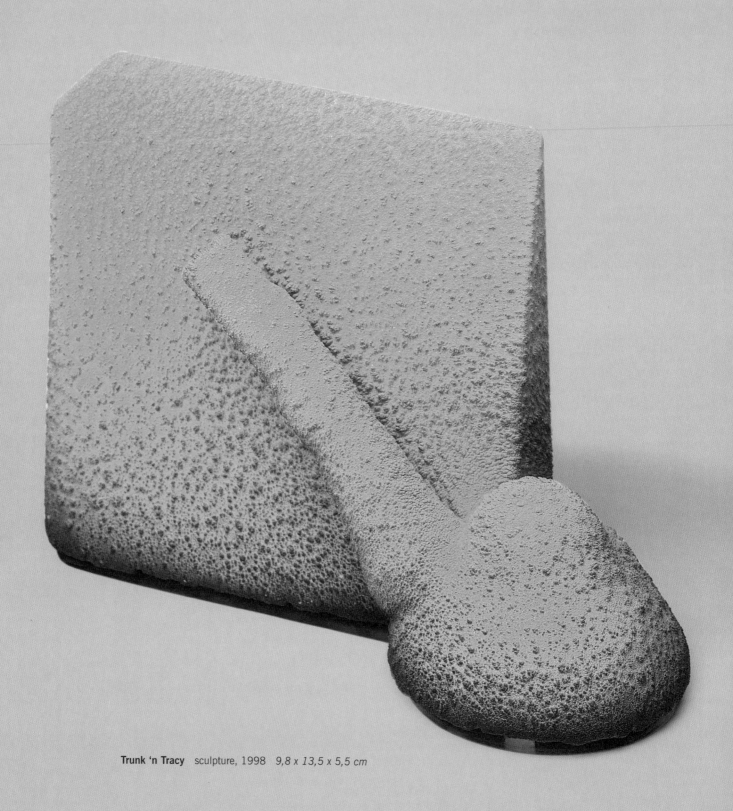

Trunk 'n Tracy   sculpture, 1998   *9,8 x 13,5 x 5,5 cm*

Rojolistic (Knob Job) sculpture, 1985 *5,7 x 11 x 4,7 cm*

untitled   vase, ca. 1900   *20 x 12 x 9 cm*

George Ohr

untitled   bowl, ca. 1900   *12 x 26 x 25,5 cm*

untitled   vase, ca. 1900   *14 x 16,5 cm*

Ken Price

Black Mound   sculpture on socle, 1961   *30,5 x 42 x 33*

Ken Price

Lou Minor Drake   vase in case, 1960   *28 x 24 x 16,5 cm*

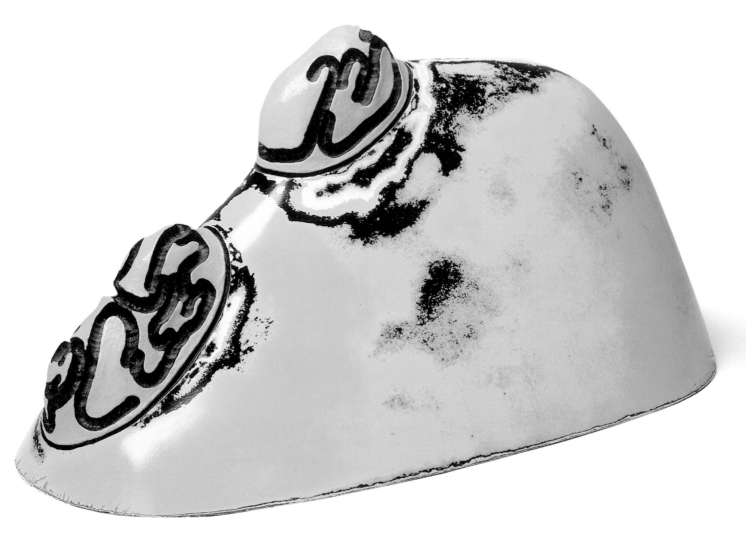

B.C. Orange   sculpture, 1967   *14,5 x 33 x 15 cm*

Ken Price

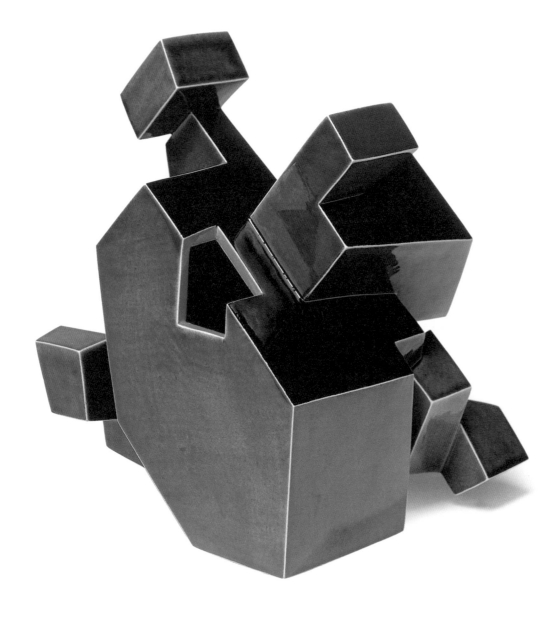

Israeli Sculpture   vase, 1979   *18 x 16,5 x 14,5 cm*

Avocado and Wine   vase, 1980   *17 x 28 x 13,5 cm*

Ken Price

Mungor   two piece sculpture, 1985   *19,8 x 19 x 18 cm*   *18,2 x 16 x 13,5 cm*

Slate Cup cup, 1972-1977 9,8 x 17 x 14,5 cm

Adrian Saxe

untitled jar, 1982 *40 x 31 cm*

Ampersand Teapot   teapot, 1988   *23 x 26 x 7 cm*

Hi-fibre 1-900-menehune magic lamp sculpture, 1997 *42 x 29 x 12 cm*

Adrian Saxe

untitled   teapot, 1994   *27 x 22 x 15 cm*

untitled   teapot, 1994   28 x 22,5 x 14,5 cm

Adrian Saxe

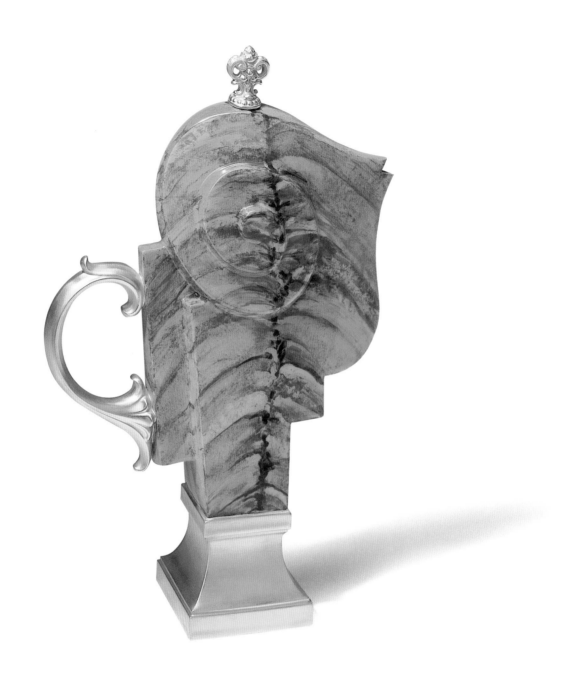

Acajou   teapot, 1992   *32 x 21 x 7,5 cm*

Circumstance of the Force du Jour   sculpture, 1996   *46 x 46,5 x 20 cm*

untitled   vase, 1939   *21,5 x 9 cm*

Light Gatherer   vase, 1988   *18,5 x 13 cm*

Rudolf Staffel

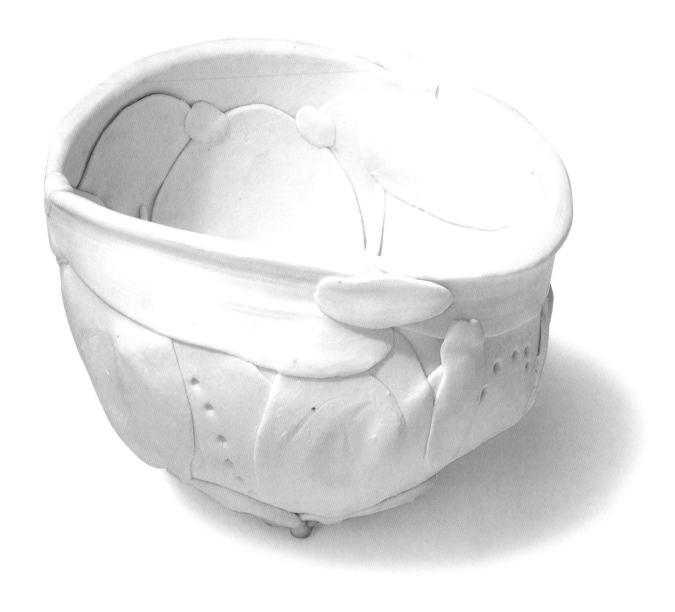

Light Gatherer   bowl, 1986   *14,5 x 22,8 x 20,5 cm*

Light Gatherer   bowl, 1985   *14,4 x 21,5 cm*

Shoreline vase, 1981 *21 x 21,5 cm*

Hi Square vase, ca. 1980-1985 *49 x 28,5 x 27 cm*

Oshobogo vase, 1986 *35,5 x 25 x 24 cm*

Akan V. vase, 1994 *55 x 38 cm*

untitled   dish, 1963   *12,4 x 32,5 x 26 cm*

untitled   pot, 1963   *34 x 24 x 17 cm*

Peter Voulkos

untitled   plate, 1963   *15 x 47,5 x 39 cm*

untitled plate, 1980 *11,5 x 50,5 x 50,5 cm*

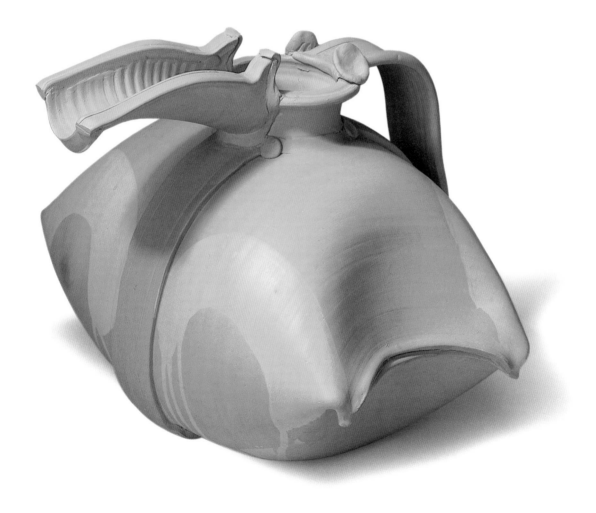

untitled 'pillow pitcher', 1981   *31 x 43 x 40 cm*

untitled multipartite sculpture, 1981 *66 x 81 x 15 cm*

Napoleon   vase on dish, 1985-1988   *24 x 35 x 14 cm*

Camillia jug, 1982 *47 x 56 x 36 cm*

Betty Woodman

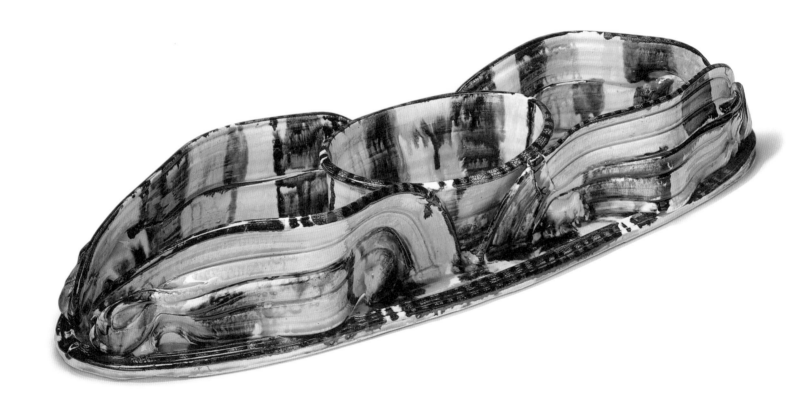

Peruvian Letter Holder   dish, 1983   *13,5 x 82 x 25 cm*

Balustrade Vase   multipartite sculpture, 1993   *150 x 120 cm*

Lindos   multipartite sculpture, 1989   *80 x 45 x 21 cm*   *57 x 52 x 23 cm*   *43 x 53 x 20 cm*

Oysterpot   vase, 1989   *77 x 53 cm*

Pistol Packing Mama   vase, 1989   *93,5 x 57 cm*

ROBERT ARNESON
1930-1992

public collections

American Craft Museum, New York, NY
Australian National Gallery, Canberra, Australia
Birmingham Museum of Art, Birmingham, AL
Des Moines Art Center, Des Moines, IA
Museum Het Kruithuis, 's-Hertogenbosch, The Netherlands
The Museum of Contemporary Art, Shigaraki Ceramic Cultural Park, Japan
Nelson-Atkins Museum of Art, Kansas City, MO
San Francisco Museum of Modern Art, San Francisco, CA
Seattle Art Museum, Seattle, WA
Stedelijk Museum, Amsterdam, The Netherlands
Whitney Museum of American Art, New York, NY

selected solo exhibitions

1997	San Francisco Museum of Modern Art, San Francisco, CA
1996	George Adams Gallery, New York, NY
1993	John Berggruen Gallery, San Francisco, CA
1992	Dorothy Goldeen Gallery, Los Angeles & Frumkins/ Adams Gallery, New York
1987	The Cleveland Museum of Art, Cleveland, Ohio
1986	Des Moines Art Center, Des Moines, IA (traveled)
1983	Landfall Press, Chicago, IL (traveled)
1982	Nelson Gallery, University of California, Davis, CA
1981	Allan Frumkin Gallery, New York, NY
1979	Moore College of Art, Philadelphia, PA
1976	Fendrick Gallery, Washington, D.C.
1975	Allan Frumkin Gallery, New York, NY
1974	Museum of Contemporary Art, Chicago, IL(traveled)
1971	Candy Store Gallery, Folsom, CA
1970	Hansen Fuller Gallery, San Francisco, CA

selected group exhibitions

1987	American Ceramics now: twenty-seventh national exhibition, Everson Museum of Art, Syracuse, New York
1983	Ceramic Echoes: historical references in contemporary ceramics, Nelson-Atkins Museum of Art, Kansas City
1981	Ceramic Sculpture: 'six artists', Whitney Museum of American Art, New York (traveled)
	The Clay Figure, American Craft Museum, New York
1980	Twenty American Artists, San Francisco Museum of Modern Art, San Francisco, CA
1979	West Coast Ceramics, Stedelijk Museum, Amsterdam, The Netherlands
	Whitney Biennial, Whitney Museum of American Art, New York
1978	Nine West Coast Sculptors, Everson Museum of Art, Syracuse, NY (traveled)
1976	Painting and Sculpture in California: The modern Era, San Francisco Museum of Modern Art, San Francisco, CA (traveled)

1974	Clay, Whitney Museum of American Art, New York, NY
	A Decade of Ceramic Art, 1962-1972, San Francisco Museum of Art, San Francisco, CA
1971	Clayworks: 20 Americans, Museum of Contemporary Crafts, New York, NY
1970	Annual Exhibition: contemporary American sculpture, Whitney Museum of American Art, New York, NY

selected bibliography

• Designed for Delight: alternative aspects of twentieth century decorative arts / ed. Martin Eidelberg. - Montreal: Montreal Museum of Decorative Arts, 1997
• Robert Arneson: Self-Reflections / essay Jonathan Fineberg. - San Francisco: San Francisco Museum of Modern Art, 1997
• 5 x 7: seven ceramic artists each acknowledge: five sources of inspiration / text Wayne Higby. - New York: Alfred University, 1993
• Catalogue of the collection 1992: The Shigaraki Ceramic Cultural Park. - Shigaraki: The Shigaraki Ceramic Cultural Park, 1993
• 30 Years of TB-9: a tribute to Robert Arneson / ed. John Natsoulas. - Davis, California: John Natsoulas Gallery, 1991
• The Book of Cups / Garth Clark. - New York: Abbeville Press Publishers, 1990
• Clay Today: contemporary ceramists and their work / Martha Drexler Lynn. - Los Angeles : Los Angeles County Museum, 1990
• American Ceramics: the collection of Everson Museum of Art / ed. Barbara Perry. - New York: Rizzoli, 1989
• Perth International Crafts Triennial / Robert Bell. - Perth: Art Gallery of Western Australia, 1989
• The History of American Ceramics: 1607 to the present, from pipkins and bean pots to contemporary forms / Elaine Levin. - New York: Harry N. Abrams, 1988
• American ceramics: 1876 to the present / Garth Clark. - New York: Abbeville Press, 1987
• American ceramics now: twenty-seventh ceramic national exhibition. - Syracuse New York: Everson Museum of Art, 1987
• Clay Revisions: plate, cup, vase / by Vicki Halper. - Seattle: Seattle Art Museum, 1987
• The new ceramics: trends and traditions / Peter Dormer. - London: Thames and Hudson, 1986
•Ceramic Echoes: historical references in contemporary ceramics / ed. Garth Clark. - Kansas City Missouri: The Contemporary Art Society, 1983
• Figurative clay sculpture Northern Californian / text Mady Jones. - San Francisco: Quay Gallery, 1982
• Centering on contemporary clay: American ceramics from the Joan Mannheimer collection / texts Jim Melchert...et.al. - Iowa City: The University of Iowa Museum of Art, 1981
• Ceramic sculpture: 'six artists' / Richard Marshall and Suzanne Foley. - New York: Whitney Museum of American Art, 1981
• Clay / curator Jacquelyn Rice. - Rhode Island: Museum of Art, 1981
• A Century of Ceramics in the United States 1878-1978: a study of its development / Garth Clark. - New York: Dutton, 1979
• Ceramics in the Pacific Northwest: a history / by LaMar Harrington. - Seattle: University of Washington Press, 1979
• Robert Arneson: Self-portraits. - Philadelphia: Moore College of Art, 1979
• West Coast ceramics: keramisch beeldhouwwerk uit de Verenigde Staten. - Amsterdam: Stedelijk Museum, 1979
• Nine West Coast clay sculptors: 1978. - Syracuse: Everson Museum of Art, 1978
•A Decade of Ceramic Art 1962-1972 / text Suzanne Foley. - San Francisco: San Francisco Museum of Art, 1972

RONALD BARON
Born 1957

CHRISTINA BERTONI
Born 1945

public collections
Museum Het Kruithuis, 's-Hertogenbosch, The Netherlands

selected solo exhibitions
1997	Anna Kustera Gallery, New York, NY
1995	Chassie Post Gallery, New York, NY
1994	Sculpture Center, New York, NY
1991	Gracie Mansion Gallery, New York, NY
1989	Milford Gallery, New York, NY
1982	Center Gallery, Madison, WI

selected group exhibitions
1999	Domestic Transformations, Brooklyn Museum, Brooklyn, NY
1998	Including Clay, Greenwich House Pottery, Jane Hartsook Gallery, New York, NYC
1997	Sculpture, James Graham Gallery, NYC
1996	Masculine Measures, Kohler Art Center, Sheboygan, WI
1994	Fever, Wexner Museum, Columbus, Ohio
1993	29th Ceramic National, Everson Museum of Art, Syracuse, NY (traveled)
1992	Al(l)ready Made, Museum Het Kruithuis, 's-Hertogenbosch, The Netherlands
1991	Thirty Years of TB-9: a tribute to Robert Arneson, Natsoulas Gallery, Davis, CA
1990	Ron Baron, Christian Marclay and Steve Wolf, Laurie Rubin Gallery, NYC
1989	The Portrait Pot, Garth Clark Gallery, New York, NY
1988	Plus Clay, Nothwest Artists Gallery, Portland, OR
1987	30 Ceramic Sculptors, Natsoulas Gallery, Davis, CA
1980	Wisconsin Biennial, Madison Art Center, Madison, WI

selected bibliography
• Trashformations. - Bellingham: Whatcom Museum of Art, 1998
• 29th Ceramic National. - Syracuse: Everson Museum of Art, 1993
• Al(l)ready Made / text Mark Kremer. - 's-Hertogenbosch: Museum Het Kruithuis, 1992
• 30 Years of TB-9: a tribute to Robert Arneson / ed. John Natsoulas. - Davis, California: John Natsoulas Gallery, 1991

public collections
E.B. Crocker Art Museum, California
Museum Het Kruithuis, 's-Hertogenbosch, The Netherlands
Museum of Fine Arts, Boston, MA

selected solo exhibitions
1993	Victoria Munroe, New York, NY
1987	Victoria Munroe, New York, NY
1985	Elliot Smith Gallery, St. Louis, MO
	Little Center Gallery, Clark University, Worcester, MA
1984	Victoria Munroe, New York, NY
1983	Impressions Gallery, Boston, MA
1981	Impressions Gallery, Boston, MA

selected group exhibitions
1990	Clay Today: contemporary ceramists and their work, Los Angeles County Art Museum, Los Angeles, CA
1989	American Clay Artists, The Port of History Museum, Philadelphia, PA
	Surface and Form, The National Museum of Ceramic Art, Baltimore, MD
1987	The Eloquent Object, Philbrook Museum of Art, Tulsa, OK (traveled)
1988	A Pot Is A Pot, Or Is It?, Athenaeum Gallery, Alexandria, VA
1986	American Pottery, Westminster Gallery, Boston, MA
	Christina Bertoni/John Gill, Pewabic Pottery, Detroit, MI
	American Potters Today, Victoria and Albert Museum, London, Great Britain
1985	Contemporary American Ceramics: twenty artists, Newport Harbor Art Museum, Newport Beach, CA
1983	Who's Afraid of American Pottery?, Museum Het Kruithuis, 's-Hertogenbosch, The Netherlands
1982	The Great American Bowl, Salve Regina College, Newport, RI

selected bibliography
• Clay Today: contemporary ceramists and their work / Martha Drexler Lynn. - Los Angeles: Los Angeles County Museum, 1990
• American Potters Today / Garth Clark and Oliver Watson. - London: Victoria and Albert Museum, 1986
• Who's afraid of American pottery? / text Evert van Straaten et al...
- 's-Hertogenbosch: Museum Het Kruithuis, 1983

KATHY BUTTERLY
Born 1963

WILLIAM DALEY
Born 1925

public collections

Museum Het Kruithuis, 's Hertogenbosch, The Netherlands
Oakland Museum of California, Oakland, CA
Renwick Gallery, National Museum of American Art, Smithsonian
Institution, Washington, D.C
The Mint Museum of Art, Charlotte, NC
University Art Museum, Arizona State University, Tempe, AZ

selected solo exhibitions

1997	Franklin Parrasch Gallery, New York, NY
1996	Franklin Parrasch Gallery, New York, NY
	Albers Fine Art Gallery, Memphis, TN
1995	Franklin Parrasch Gallery, New York, NY
1994	Franklin Parrasch Gallery, New York, NY
	Nancy Margolis Gallery, New York, NY
1993	The Clay Studio, Philadelphia, PA
1992	Moore College of Art, Philadelphia, PA

selected group exhibitions

1997	Forms and Transformations of Clay, Queens Borough Public Library Gallery, Jamaica, NY
1995-96	New York, NY: Clay, Nordenfjeldeske Kunstindustrimuseum, Trondheim, Norway
1994-95	Robert Arneson-changing the face of American Ceramics: a tribute, Kingsborough Community College, Brooklyn, NY
1994	Albers Fine Art Gallery, Memphis, TN
	Talentborse Handwerk 1994, Munich, Germany
1993	Kathy Butterly, Jeffrey Chap, Steven Fedrick-new ceramic works, Archon Gallery, New York, NY
1992	Contemporary Ceramics, Bennington College Gallery, Bennington, VT
1991	Thirty years of TB-9: a tribute to Robert Arneson, John Natsoulas Gallery, Davis, CA
	The 47th Scripps Ceramic Annual, Lang Gallery, Scripps College, Claremont, CA
1990	The Fourth Concorso Nazionale della Ceramica d' Arte: Savona-Fortezza Primiar, Savona, Italy

selected bibliography

• Kathy Butterly: recent works.- New York: Franklin Parrasch Gallery, 1997
• 30 Years of TB-9: a tribute to Robert Arneson / ed. John Natsoulas.-
Davis, California: John Natsoulas Gallery, 1991

public collections

American Craft Museum, New York, NY
Cambell Museum, Camden, NJ
Everson Museum of Art, Syracuse, NY
Museum Het Kruithuis, 's-Hertogenbosch, The Netherlands
National Museum of American Art-Smithonian Institute, Washington, D.C
The National Museum of Contemporary Art, Seoul, Korea
Philadelphia Museum of Art, Philadelphia, PA
The Saint Louis Museum of Art, St. Louis, MO
Victoria and Albert Museum, London, Great Britain

selected solo exhibitions

1993	The Levy Gallery for the Arts, Philadelphia, PA (traveled)
1990	Helen Drutt Gallery, New York, NY
	University of the Arts, Philadelphia, PA
	Helen Drutt Gallery, New York, NY
1988	Chicago International New Art Forms Exposition, Chicago, IL
	Helen Drutt Gallery, Philadelphia, PA
1985	Braunstein Gallery, San Francisco, CA
	Garth Clark Gallery, New York, NY
	Fosdick Nelson Gallery, Alfred University, NY and Pewabic Society Gallery, Detroit, MI
1982	Carreiro Gallery, Massachusetts College of Art, Boston, MA
	Helen Drutt Gallery, Philadelphia, PA
1981	Exhibit A, Chicago, IL
1980	Helen Drutt Gallery, Philadelphia, PA
1979	Braunstein Quay Gallery, San Francisco, CA
1976	Helen Drutt Gallery, Philadelphia, PA
1974	Helen Drutt Gallery, Philadelphia, PA

selected group exhibitions

1993	The Art of Craft, Boca Raton Museum of Art, Boca Raton, FL
	Daley/Vaskys Reinhardt, Haviland Strickland Gallery, University of the Arts, Philadelphia. PA
1992	Contemporary Crafts by Pennsylvania Artists, The University Museum, Indiana University of Pennsylvania, Indiana, PA
	A Decade of Craft: recent acquisitions, American Craft Museum, New York, NY
1991	Functional Ceramics 1991, Wayne Center for the Arts, Wooster, Ohio
1989	Craft Today-U.S.A, Musée des Arts Décoratifs Paris, France (traveled)
	American Clay Artists 1989, Clay Studio, Port of History Museum, Philadelphia, PA
1987	American Ceramics Now: the twenty-seventh ceramic national exhibition, Everson Museum of Art, Syracuse, NY
1986	American Potters Today, Victoria and Albert Museum, London, Great Britain
	Contemporary Arts: an expanding view, The Monmouth Museum

of Art, Monmouth, NJ
Contemporary American Ceramics, The National Museum of
Contemporary Arts, Seoul, Korea
1983   Three Person Exhibition, Betty Woodman/Elsa Rady/William
Daley, Douglas Drake Gallery, Kansas City, MO
Ceramic Echoes: historical references in contemporary ceramics,
Nelson-Atkins Museum of Art, Kansas City, MO
Who's Afraid of American Pottery?, Museum Het Kruithuis,
's-Hertogenbosch, The Netherlands
American Clay Artists, Clay Studio, Philadelphia, PA
1981   American Ceramics from the Joan Mannheimer Collection,
University of Iowa Museum, Iowa City, IA
1980   The Contemporary American Potter, University of Northern Iowa,
Cedar Falls, IA
1979   A Century of Ceramics in the USA, Everson Museum of Art,
Syracuse, NY
1977   The Ceramic Vessel as Metaphor, The Evanston Art Center,
Evanston, IL
1975   Three Centuries of American Art in Philadelphia, Philadelphia
Museum of Art, Philadelphia, PA

selected bibliography

• William Daley: ceramic works and drawings / text Matthew Drutt...et al. -
Philadelphia: Levy Gallery for the Arts, 1993
• International Crafts / ed. Martina Margetts. - London: Thames and
Hudson, 1991
• William P. Daley 1990-1980. - Philadelphia: The University of the Arts,
1990
• American Clay Artists 1989 / text Jimmy Clark...et al. - Philadelphia:
Port of History Museum, 1989
• American Ceramics: 1876 to the present / Garth Clark. - New York:
Abbeville Press, 1987
• American Ceramics Now: twenty-seventh ceramic national exhibition. -
Syracuse New York: Everson Museum of Art, 1987
• The New Ceramics / Peter Dormer. - London: Thames and Hudson, 1986
• Ceramic Echoes: historical references in contemporary ceramics / ed.
Garth Clark. - Kansas City Missouri: The Contemporary Art Society, 1983
• Who's Afraid of American Pottery? / text Evert van Straaten...et al. -
's-Hertogenbosch: Museum Het Kruithuis, 1983
• William Daley: selected works 1954-1982. - Boston: Carreiro Gallery,
1982
• American Potters: the work of twenty modern masters / Garth Clark. -
New York: Watson-Guptill, 1981
• Centering on contemporary clay: American ceramics from the Joan
Mannheimer collection / text Jim Melchert...et al. - Iowa City: The
University of Iowa Museum of Art, 1981
• The Ceramic Vessel as Metaphor: sixth national ceramics invitational. -
Evanston: Art Center, 1977
• Philadelphia: three centuries of American art. - Philadelphia: Philadelphia
Museum of Art, 1976

RICHARD DEVORE
Born 1933

public collections

American Craft Museum, New York, NY
Arkansas Art Center, Little Rock, AR
Cleveland Art Museum, Cleveland, OH
Delaware Art Museum, Wilmington, DE
Denver Art Museum, Denver, CO
Everson Museum of Art, Syracuse, NY
Los Angeles County Museum of Art, Los Angeles, CA
Metropolitan Museum of Art, New York, NY
Museum Boijmans van Beuningen, Rotterdam, The Netherlands
Museum Het Kruithuis, 's-Hertogenbosch, The Netherlands
National Collection of Contemporary Art at the Louvre, Paris, France
National Museum of American Art, Washington, DC
Nelson-Atkins Museum of Art, Kansas City, MO
Newark Museum, Newark, NJ
Philadelphia Museum of Art, Philadelphia, PA
Victoria and Albert Museum, London, Great Britain

selected solo exhibitions

1999   Frank Lloyd Gallery, Santa Monica, CA
1996   Max Protetch Gallery, New York, NY
1994   Max Protetch Gallery, New York, NY
1993   Garth Clark Gallery, Los Angeles, CA
      Bellas Artes Gallery, Santa Fe, NM
1992   Locks Gallery, Philadelphia, PA
1991   Max Protetch Gallery, New York
1988   Greenberg Gallery, St. Louis, MO
1985   Exhibit A Gallery, Chicago, IL
1984   Hill Gallery, Birmingham, MI
1983   Milwaukee Art Museum, WI (traveled)
1980   Okun-Thomas Gallery, St. Louis, MO
1979   Drutt Gallery, Philadelphia, PA
1978   Freudenheim Gallery, Buffalo, NY
1977   Fendrick Gallery, Washington, DC
1976   Quay Gallery, San Francisco, CA
1975   Yaw Gallery, Birmingham, MI
1974   Cranbrook Academy of Art Museum, Bloomfield Hills, MI

selected group exhibitions

1995   Material Nature: process/product, Sun Valley Center for the Arts,
Ketchum, ID
1994   Masterworks of Ceramic Art - historic and contemporary,
Newark Museum of Art, Newark, NJ
1993   New Acquisitions: craft today, USA, American Craft Museum,
New York, NY
1992   Contemporary Clay: five artists, Greenberg Gallery, St. Louis, MO
1991   Recent Fires: contemporary American ceramics, Utah Museum
of Fine Art, Salt Lake City, UT (traveled)
1990   28th Ceramic National Exhibition, Everson Museum of Art,

Syracuse, New York (traveled)
DeVore, Price, Turner, Hill Gallery, Birmingham, MI
1987 The Eloquent Object, The Philbrook Museum of Art, Tulsa, OK (traveled)
   American Ceramics Now, Everson Museum of Art, Syracuse, NY (traveled)
1986 Craft Today: poetry of the physical, American Craft Museum, New York, NY (traveled)
   American Potters Today, Victoria and Albert Museum, London, Great Britain
1985 Clay - 28 American artists, The Dayton Art Institute, Dayton, OH
1983 Who's Afraid of American Pottery? Museum Het Kruithuis, 's-Hertogenbosch, The Netherlands
   Ceramic Echoes: historical references in contemporary ceramics, Nelson Atkins Museum, Kansas City, MO
1979 A Century of Ceramics in the United States, Everson Museum of Art, Syracuse, NY (traveled)
1977 The Ceramic Vessel as Metaphor, Evanston Art Center, Evanston, IL
1976 Amercan Crafts: an aesthetic view, Museum of Contemporary Art, Chicago, IL
1975 Clay U.S.A Fendrick Gallery, Washington, DC
1972 International Invitational, Victoria and Albert Museum, London, Great Britain

selected bibliography

• Au-delà de la tradition: la collection de céramique contemporaine du Musée Boijmans van Beuningen Rotterdam. - Paris: Institut Néerlandais, 1992
• International Crafts / ed. by Martina Margetts. - London: Thames and Hudson, 1991
• Clay Today: contemporary ceramists and their work / Martha Drexler Lynn. - Los Angeles : Los Angeles County Museum, 1990
• American ceramics: the collection of Everson Museum of Art / ed. Barabara Perry. - New York: Rizzoli 1989
• American ceramics now: twenty-seventh ceramic national exhibition. - Syracuse New York: Everson Museum of Art, 1987
• The New Ceramics: trends and traditions / Peter Dormer. - London: Thames and Hudson, 1986
• Ceramic Echoes: historical references in contemporary ceramics/ Garth Clark . - Kansas City Missouri: The Contemporary Art Society, 1983
• Who's afraid of American Pottery? / text Evert van Straaten...et al. - 's-Hertogenbosch: Museum Het Kruithuis, 1983
• American potters: the work of twenty modern masters / Garth Clark. - New York: Watson-Guptill, 1981
• Richard Devore: pottery. - Chicago: Exhibit A, 1981
• The Contemporary American Potter: recent vessels / essays Garth Clark and Sanford Sivitz Shaman. - Cedar Falls: University of Northern Iowa, 1980

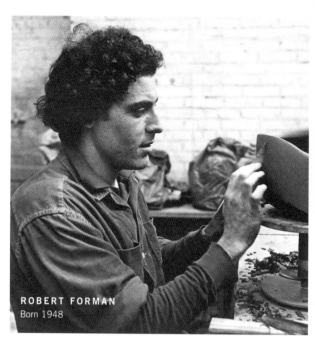

ROBERT FORMAN
Born 1948

public collections
Museum Het Kruithuis, 's-Hertogenbosch, The Netherlands

selected solo exhibitions
1981 Museum Het Kruithuis, 's-Hertogenbosch, The Netherlands
   Galerie Het Kapelhuis, Amersfoort, The Netherlands
   Helen Drutt Gallery, Philadelphia. PA

selected group exhibitions
1982 Who's afraid of American Pottery?, Museum Het Kruithuis, 's-Hertogenbosch, The Netherlands
1983 Young Americans: clay/glass, American Craft Museum, New York, NY

selected bibliography
• Who's afraid of American Pottery?/ text Evert van Straaten...et al. - 's-Hertogenbosch: Museum Het Kruithuis, 1983
• Robert Forman / text Evert van Straaten. - 's-Hertogenbosch: Museum Het Kruithuis, 1981

VIOLA FREY
Born 1933

public collections

The American Craft Museum, New York, NY
The Arkansas Arts Center, Little Rock, AR
The Detroit Institute of Arts, Detroit, MI
Everson Museum of Art, Syracuse, NY
Los Angeles County Museum of Art, Los Angeles, CA
Minneapolis Institute of the Arts, Minneapolis, MN
Museum Het Kruithuis, 's-Hertogenbosch, The Netherlands
Oakland Museum, Oakland, CA
Philadelphia Museum of Art, Philadelphia, PA
The Saint Louis Art Museum, St. Louis, MO
San Francisco Museum of Modern Art, San Francisco, CA
The Shigaraki Ceramic Cultural Park, Shigaraki, Japan
Whitney Museum of American Art, New York, NY

selected solo exhibitions

1998	Rena Bransten Gallery, San Francisco, CA
1997	Frank Lloyd Gallery, Santa Monica, CA
1994	The Butler Institute of American Art, Youngstown, OH (traveled)
1992	Crocker Museum of Art, Sacramento, CA
1988	Rena Bransten Gallery, San Francisco, CA
1987	Nancy Hoffman Gallery, New York, NY
1986	Asher/Faure Gallery, Los Angeles, CA
1985	Rena Bransten Quay Gallery, San Francisco, CA
1984	Whitney Museum of American Art, New York, NY
	Moore College of Art, Philadelhpia, PA (traveled)
1983	The Charles H. Scott Gallery, Emily Carr College of Art, Grandville Island, Vancouver, Canada
	Quay Gallery, San Francisco, CA
1982	Fullerton Art Gallery, California State University, Fullerton, CA
1981	Crocker Art Museum, Sacramento, CA (traveled)
1980	Quay Gallery, San Francisco, CA
1977	Wenger Gallery, La Jolla, CA
1975	Hank Baum Gallery, San Francisco, CA
1974	Wenger Gallery, San Francisco, CA

selected group exhibitions

1998	20/20 The 20th Anniversary Exhibition, University Art Gallery, Sonoma State University, Sonoma, CA
1997	The Hirshhorn Collects: recent acquisitions 1992-1996, Hirshhorn Museum and Sculpture Garden, Smithsonian Institution, Washington, District of Columbia
1996	Ceramic Sculpture from the East Bay, California State University, Hayward, CA
1995	In Three Dimensions: women sculptors of the 90's, Newhouse Center for Contemporary Art, Snug Harbor Cultural Center, Staten Island, NY
1994	Breaking Barriers, American Craft Museum, New York, NY (traveled)
1993	Modernism: Craft Breakthrough in Northern California, 1950-1975, California Crafts Museum, San Francisco, CA
1992	The Figure: two bay area artists: Christopher Brown and Viola Frey, Johnson County Community College, Gallery of Art, Overland Park, MO
1991	Experiencing Sculpture: the figure in American art, Hudson River

	Museum, Yonkers, NY
1990	American Ceramic Sculpture, The National Museum of Ceramic Art, Baltimore, MD
1989	Craft Today: U.S.A., American Craft Museum, New York, NY (traveled)
	Summer Pleasures: Water, Nancy Hoffman Gallery, New York, NY
	Urban Figures, Whitney Museum of American Art at Philip Morris, New York, NY
1987	Quatre Americains à la Manufacture de Sèvres, American Center, Paris, France
	American Ceramics Now: The twenty-seventh ceramic national exhibition, Everson Museum of Art, Syracuse, NY
	Clay Revisions: plate, cup and vase, Seattle Art Museum, Seattle, WA (traveled)
1986	Contemporary American Studio Pottery: an overview, Victoria and Albert Museum, London, Great Britain
	Craft Today: poetry of the physical, American Craft Museum, New York, NY (traveled)
1985	American Clay Artists: Philadelphia '85, Port of History Museum, Philadelphia, PA
	Art in the San Francisco Bay Area, 1945-1980, The Oakland Museum, Oakland, CA
	Recent Ceramic Sculpture, University Art Museum, University of New Mexico
1984	Figurative Sculpture: ten artists/two decades, University Art Museum, California State University- Long Beach, Long Beach, CA
	The 20th Century: The San Francisco Museum of Modern Art Collection, San Francisco Museum of Modern Art, San Francisco, CA
1983	Ceramic Echoes: historical references in contemporary ceramics, Nelson-Atkins Museum of Art, Kansas City, MO
	The Raw Edge: ceramics of the 80's, Hillwood Art Gallery, Long Island University, Greenvale, NY
1982	Clay Bodies: Autio, DeStaebler & Frey, Maryland Institute, College of Art, Baltimore, MD
	Figurative Clay, Quay Gallery, San Francisco, CA
1981	The Clay Figure, Museum of Contemporary Crafts, New York, NY
1979	Century of Ceramics in the United States, Everson Museum of Art, Syracuse, NY
1977	Ceramic Invitational, Sacramento, CA

selected bibliography

• Viola Frey / text Reena Jana. - San Francisco: Rena Bransten Gallery, 1998
• Viola Frey: Arguments. - San Francisco: Rena Bransten Gallery, 1995
• Catalogue of the collection 1992: The Shigaraki Ceramic Cultural Park. - Shigaraki: The Shigaraki Ceramic Cultural Park, 1993
• International Crafts / ed. Martina Margetts. - London: Thames and Hudson, 1991
• Clay Today: contemporary ceramists and their work / Martha Drexler Lynn. - Los Angeles: Los Angeles County Museum, 1990
• Manufacture Nationale de Sèvres 1740 - 1990. - Sèvres: Manufacture nationale de Sèvres, 1990
• Viola Frey - San Francisco: Rena Bransten Gallery, 1990
• American Ceramics: the collection of Everson Museum of Art / ed. Barbara Perry. - New York: Rizzoli, 1989
• The History of American Ceramics: 1607 to the present, from pipkins and bean pots to contemporary forms / Elaine Levin. - New York: Harry N. Abrams, 1988
• American Ceramics: 1876 to the present / Garth Clark. - New York: Abbeville Press, 1987
• American Ceramics Now: twenty-seventh ceramic international exhibition / Syracuse New York: Everson Museum of Art, 1987
• Clay Revisions: plate, cup, vase / by Vicki Halper. - Seattle: Seattle Art Museum, 1987
• The new ceramics: trends and traditions/ Peter Dormer - London: Thames and Hudson, 1986
• Ceramic Echoes: historical references in contemporary ceramics / ed. Garth Clark. - Kansas City Missouri: The Contemporary Art Society, 1983
• The raw edge: ceramics of the 80's. - New York: Hillwood Art Gallery, 1983
• Viola Frey: retrospective / essay Garth Clark. - Sacramento: Creative Arts League, 1981

ANDREA GILL
Born 1948

public collections
Los Angeles County Museum, Los Angeles, CA
Museum Het Kruithuis, 's-Hertogenbosch, The Netherlands
New York State College of Ceramics at Alfred University, Alfred, NY
Philadelphia Museum of Art, Philadelphia, PA
Victoria and Albert Museum, London, Great Britain

selected solo exhibitions
1993   Okun Gallery, Santa Fe, New Mexico
1992   Swidler Gallery, Royal Oak, MI
1988   Hinkle Memorial Library, Alfred State College, Alfred, NY
1985   DBR Gallery, Cleveland, OH
1984   The Elements Gallery, New York, NY
1983   Garth Clark Gallery, Los Angeles, CA
1982   The Elements Gallery, New York, NY
1981   Akron Art Museum, Akron, OH
1980   The Evanston Art Center, Octagon Gallery, Evanston, IL
1978   Sheridan Inn Gallery, Sheridan, WY

selected group exhibitions
1995   In Praise of Craft, National Museum of American Art, Washington, D.C.
1993   Contemporary Crafts and the Saxe Collection, The Toledo Museum of Art, Toledo, OH
1990   The Figure, National Ceramic Museum, Baltimore, MD
1989   The Alfred Show, Dorothy Weiss Gallery, San Francisco, CA
        Forms and Surface, National Museum of Ceramic Art, Baltimore, MD
1988   Is It a Pot...or Not?, The Atheneum Museum, Alexandria, VA
1987   Clay Revisions: plate, cup, vase, Seattle Art Museum, Seattle, WA (traveled)
1986   Craft Today: poetry of the physical, American Craft Museum, New York, NY
        American Potters Today, Victoria and Albert Museum, London, Great Britain
        Contemporary Arts: an expanding view, The Monmouth Museum, Lincroft, NJ
1985   Painted Pottery: continuing the tradition of tin glazed earthenware, Glendon Gallery, Toronto, Canada
        Contemporary American Ceramics: twenty artists, Newport Harbor Art Museum, Newport, RI
1984   Image/Vessel/Image, Garth Clark Gallery, New York, NY
1983   Ceramic Echoes: historical references in contemporary ceramics, Nelson-Atkins Museum of Art, Kansas City, MO
1982   Figurative Clay, Garth Clark Gallery, Los Angeles, CA
1981   Beyond Tradition: 25th anniversary show, American Craft Museum, New York, NY
        Centering on Contemporary Ceramics: The Joan Mannheimer Collection, University of Iowa Museum, Iowa City, IA

1980   Contemporary Ceramics: a response to Wedgwood, Museum of the Philadelphia Civic Center
1979   American Ceramics, Helen Drutt Gallery, Philadelphia, PA
1978   Young Americans: clay/glass, American Crafts Council, Museum of Contemporary Crafts, New York, NY

selected bibliography
• Anne Currier - Val M. Cushing - Andrea Gill / text Nancy Weekly. - New York: Division of Ceramic Art, New York State College at Alfred University, 1996
• Alfred teaches ceramics, 1900-1996 / compiled and ed. Margaret Carney. - New York: Museum of Ceramic Art at Alfred, 1996
• The White House Collection of American Crafts / text Michael W. Monroe. - New York: Harry N. Abrams, 1995
• Alfred now: contemporary American ceramics / Donald Kuspit and Nancy Weekly. - Champaign, Illinois: Krannert Art Museum and Kinkead Pavilion, 1994
• Clay Today: contemporary ceramists and their work / Martha Drexler Lynn. - Los Angeles: Los Angeles County Museum, 1990
• The History of American Ceramics: 1607 to the present, from pipkins and bean pots to contemporary forms / Elaine Levin . - New York: Harry N. Abrams, 1988
• American ceramics: 1876 to the present / Garth Clark. - New York: Abbeville Press, 1987
• Clay Revisions: plate, cup, vase / by Vicki Halper. - Seattle: Seattle Art Museum, 1987
• Painted Clay / text Jos Poodt. - 's-Hertogenbosch: Museum Het Kruithuis, 1987
• The new ceramics: trends and traditions / Peter Dormer. - London: Thames and Hudson, 1986.
• Ceramic Echoes: historical references in contemporary ceramics / ed. Garth Clark. - Kansas City Missouri: The Contemporary Art Society, 1983
• Who's afraid of American pottery? / text Evert van Straaten...et al. - 's-Hertogenbosch: Museum Het Kruithuis, 1983

DAVID GILHOOLY
Born 1943

WAYNE HIGBY
Born 1943

public collections

Everson Museum of Art, Syracuse, NY

Museum Het Kruithuis, 's-Hertogenbosch, The Netherlands

Museum of Contemporary Crafts, New York, NY

Oakland Art Museum, Oakland, CA

selected group exhibitions

1981   Ceramic Sculpture: 'six artists', Whitney Museum of American
        Art, New York, NY

1971   Clayworks: 20 Americans, Museum of Contemporary Crafts,
        New York, NY

selected bibliography

• An Industrious Art: innovation in pattern and print at the Fabric Workshop
/ ed. Marion Boulton Stroud. - Philadelphia : The Fabric Workshop, 1991

• American Ceramics: the collection of Everson Museum of Art / ed.
Barbara Perry. - New York : Rizzoli, 1989

• American ceramics: 1876 to the present / Garth Clark. - New York:
Abbeville Press, 1987

• The new ceramics: trends and traditions / Peter Dormer. - London:
Thames and Hudson, 1986.

• Ceramic sculpture: 'six artists' / Richard Marshall and Suzanne Foley. -
New York: Whitney Museum of American Art, 1981

• Nine West Coast Clay Sculptors: 1978. - Syracuse: Everson Museum of
Art, 1978

• Clay USA. - Washington DC: Fendrick Gallery, 1975

• A Decade of Ceramic Art 1962-1972 / text Suzanne Foley. -
San Francisco: San Francisco Museum of Art, 1972

• Clayworks: 20 Americans. - New York: Museum of Contemporary Crafts,
1971

public collections

American Craft Museum, New York, NY

Boston Museum of Fine Arts, Boston, MA

Brooklyn Museum of Art, Brooklyn, NY

Carnegie Museum of Art, Pittsburgh, PA

Denver Art Museum, Denver, CO

Everson Museum of Art, Syracuse, NY

Honolulu Academy of Art, Honolulu, HI

Los Angeles County Museum of Art, Los Angeles, CA

Metropolitan Museum of Art, New York, NY

Minneapolis Institute of Arts, Minneapolis, MN

Museum Het Kruithuis, 's-Hertogenbosch, The Netherlands

National Museum of American Art, Smithsonian Institution, Washington, D.C

National Museum of Modern Art, Tokyo, Japan

Philadelphia Museum of Art, Philadelphia, PA

Victoria and Albert Museum, London, Great Britain

selected solo exhibitions

1991   Morgan Gallery, Kansas City, MO

1990   Helen Drutt Gallery, New York, NY

1988   Helen Drutt Gallery, New York, NY

1984   Greenwich House Pottery, New York, NY

1979   Okun -Thomas Gallery, St. Louis, MO

1980   Helen Drutt Gallery, Philadelphia, PA

1978   Exhibit A, Chicago, IL

1973   American Craft Museum, New York, NY

1971   Benson Gallery, Bridgehampton, NY

selected group exhibitions

1995   Kaolin International Ceramic Art Exhibition, Jianxi Porcelain
        Research Institute, Jingdezhen, China

1993   New Acquisitions, National Museum of Modern Art, Tokyo, Japan

1992   Twentieth Century Ceramics, Los Angeles County Museum of
        Art, Los Angeles, CA

1991   Seventeen Years 1974-1991, Helen Drutt Gallery, Philadelphia, PA

1989   Fragile Blossoms, Enduring Earth: The Japanese influence on
        American ceramics, Everson Museum of Art, Syracuse, NY

1988   Power Over the Clay: American studio potters, Detroit Institute
        of Arts, Detroit, MI

1987   The Eloquent Object, Philbrook Museum of Art, Tulsa, OK
        (traveled)
        American Ceramics Now: twenty-seventh ceramic national
        exhibition, Everson Museum of Art, Syracuse, NY

1986   Craft Today: poetry of the physical, American Craft Museum,
        New York, NY (traveled)
        American Potters Today, Victoria and Albert Museum, London,
        Great Britain

1985   International Ceramics, Taipei Fine Arts Museum, Taiwan, China

1984   Clay Vessels: works by 10 modern masters, Palo Alto Cultural

Center, Palo Alto, CA

1983 Ceramic Echoes: historical references in contemporary
ceramics, Nelson-Atkins Museum, Kansas City, MO

1981 Centering on Contemporary Clay: American ceramics from the
Joan Mannheimer Collection, Museum of Art, University of
Iowa, Iowa City

1977 The Ceramic Vessel as Metaphor, Evanston Art Center,
Evanston, IL

1972 International Ceramics, Victoria and Albert Museum, London,
Great Britain

selected bibliography

• Alfred teaches ceramics, 1900-1996 / ed. Margaret Carney. - New York :
Museum of Ceramic Art at Alfred, 1996
• Alfred Now: contemporary American ceramics / Donald Kuspit & Nancy
Weekly. - Champaign : Krannert Art Museum and Kinkead Pavilion, 1994
• International Crafts / ed. Martina Margetts. - London : Thames and
Hudson, 1991
• Wayne Higby / text Robert Turner. - New York : Helen Drutt Gallery, 1990
• American Ceramics: the collection of Everson Museum of Art / ed.
Barbara Perry. - New York : Rizzoli, 1989
• The History of American Ceramics: 1607 to the present, from pipkins
and bean pots to contemporary forms / Elaine Levin. - New York : Harry N.
Abrams, 1988
• American Ceramics: 1876 to the present / Garth Clark. - New York :
Abbeville Press, 1987
• American Ceramics Now: twenty-seventh ceramic national exhibition. -
Syracuse : Everson Museum of Art, 1987
• The New Ceramics: trends and traditions / Peter Dormer. - London :
Thames and Hudson, 1986
• Ceramic Echoes: historical references in contemporary ceramics / ed.
Garth Clark. - Kansas City : The Contemporary Art Society, 1983
• Master Craftsmen. - Jacksonville : Jacksonville Art Museum, 1982
• Centering on contemporary clay: American ceramics from the Joan
Mannheimer collection / texts Jim Melchert...et al. - Iowa City :
The University of Iowa Museum of Art, 1981

GRAHAM MARKS
Born 1951

public collections

American Craft Museum, New York, NY
Museum Het Kruithuis, 's-Hertogenbosch, The Netherlands
Cranbrook Academy of Art Museum, Bloomfield Hills, MI
Everson Museum of Art, Syracuse, NY
Museum of Art, University of Iowa, Iowa City

selected solo exhibitions

1986 Everson Museum of Art, Syracuse, NY
1981 John Michael Kohler Arts Center, Sheboygan, WI

selected group exhibitions

1988 Power Over the Clay-American Studio Potters, Detroit Institute of
Art, Detroit, MI

1987 What's New?, American Ceramics since 1980, The Alfred and
Mary Shands Collection, J.B Speed Museum of Art, Louisville, KY

1986 Craft Today: poetry of the physical, American Craft Museum,
New York, NY (traveled)
Contemporary Arts: an expanding view, Monmouth Museum of
Art, Lincroft, NJ

1985 Contemporary American Ceramics: twenty artists, Newport
Harbor Art Museum, CA

1983 Who's Afraid of American Pottery?, Museum Het Kruithuis,
's-Hertogenbosch, The Netherlands

1982 Young Americans- Award Winners, American Craft Museum,
New York, NY

1981 Beyond Tradition- 25th Anniversary Exhibition, American Craft
Museum, NY
Centering on Contemporary Clay- Ceramics from the Joan
Mannheimer Collection, University of Iowa, Iowa City

1980 Ceramic Sculpture, Kansas City Art Institute, MO

1977 The Ceramic Vessel as Metaphor, Evanston Art Center, Evanston, IL

1975 Supermud Invitational, Carborundum, Museum of Ceramics,
Niagara Falls, NY

selected bibliography

• An Industrious Art: innovation in pattern and print at the Fabric Workshop
/ ed. Marion Boulton Stroud. - Philadelphia: The Fabric Workshop, 1991
• Clay, Color, Content: the 28th ceramic national / ed. Thomas Piché. -
Syracuse: Everson Museum of Art, 1990
• American ceramics: the collection of Everson Museum of Art / ed.
Barbara Perry. - New York: Rizzoli, 1989
• American ceramics: 1876 to the present / Garth Clark. - New York:
Abbeville Press, 1987
• The New Ceramics: trends and traditions / Peter Dormer. - London:
Thames and Hudson, 1986
• Who's afraid of American Pottery? / text Evert van Straaten...et al. -
's-Hertogenbosch: Museum Het Kruithuis, 1983
• The ceramic vessel as metaphor: sixth national ceramics invitational. -
Evanston: Evanston Art Center, 1977

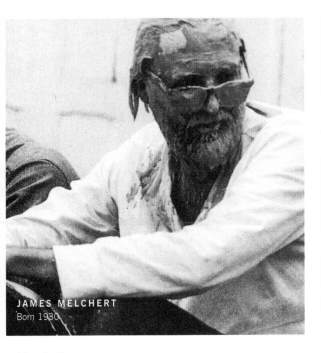

JAMES MELCHERT
Born 1930

RON NAGLE
Born 1939

public collections
Museum Het Kruithuis, 's-Hertogenbosch, The Netherlands
Museum of Contemporary Crafts, New York, NY
San Francisco Museum of Art, San Francisco, CA
Victoria and Albert Musuem, London, Great Britain

selected solo exhibitions
1992	The Fabric Workshop, Philadelphia, PA
1991	Holly Solomon Gallery, NY
	Kala Institute, Berkeley, CA
1990	Grey Gallery, East Carolina State, Greenville
1989	College of Notre Dame, Belmont, CA
1984	Fuller Goldeen Gallery, San Francisco, CA
1981	The Fendrick Gallery, Washington, DC
1975	Museum of Modern Art, San Francisco, CA
1970	San Francisco Art Institute, CA

selected group exhibitions
1993	California Eclectic, Trans-America Pyramid, San Francisco, CA
1991	The Projected Image, Museum of Modern Art, San Francisco, CA
1987	The Precious Object, Oakland Museum, Oakland, CA
1986	Sculpture from the Museum Collection, Museum of Modern Art, San Francisco, CA
1977	California Painting and Sculpture, National Museum of American Art, Washington, D.C.
1972	Contemporary Ceramic Art, National Museum of Modern Art, Kyoto, Japan

selected bibliography
• The History of American Ceramics: 1607 to the present, from pipkins and bean pots to contemporary forms / Elaine Levin. - New York: Harry N. Abrams, 1988
• American ceramics: 1876 to the present / Garth Clark. - New York: Abbeville Press, 1987
• A Decade of Ceramic Art 1962-1972 / text Suzanne Foley. - San Francisco: San Francisco Museum of Art, 1972
• Clayworks: 20 Americans. - New York: Museum of Contemporary Crafts, 1971

public collections
Everson Museum of Art, Syracuse, New York, NY
Los Angeles County Museum, Los Angeles, LA
Museum Het Kruithuis, 's-Hertogenbosch, The Netherlands
Newport Harbor Art Museum, Newport Beach, CA
Oakland Museum, Oakland, CA
Philadelphia Museum of Art, Philadelphia, PA
Rhode Island School of Design, Providence, RI
Saint Louis Museum of Art, St. Louis, MO
San Francisco Museum of Modern Art, San Francisco, CA
Stedelijk Museum, Amsterdam, The Netherlands
Utah Museum of Fine Arts, Salt Lake City, UT
Victoria and Albert Museum, London, Great Britain

selected solo exhibitions
1998	Garth Clark Gallery, New York, NY
1996	Revolution, Ferndale, MI
1995	Franklin Parrasch Gallery, New York, NY
1994	The Carnegie Museum of Art, Pittsburgh, PA
1993	Mills College Art Gallery, Oakland, CA
1992	Bella Artes Gallery, Santa Fe, New Mexico
1991	Rena Bransten Gallery, San Francisco, CA
1989	Charles Cowles Gallery, New York, NY
1988	Rena Bransten Gallery, San Francisco, CA
1985	Charles Cowles Gallery, New York, NY
1984	Betsy Rosenfeld Gallery, Chicago, IL
1983	Charles Cowles Gallery, New York, NY
1981	Charles Cowles Gallery, New York, NY
1979	Saint Louis Art Museum, St. Louis, MO
1978	Adaline Kent Award Exhibition, San Francisco Art Institute, San Francisco, CA
1975	Quay Gallery, San Francisco, CA

selected group exhibitions
1998	Clay into Art, Metropolitan Museum of Art, New York, NY
1997	Celebrating American Craft: American Craft 1975- 1995, The Danish Museum of Decorative Art, Copenhagen, Denmark
	Abstract Expressionist Ceramics: myth and reality revisited, Garth Clark Gallery, New York, NY
	The Renwick at 25, Renwick Gallery of the National Museum of American Art, Smithsonian Institution, Washington DC
1996	Clay: Recent Ceramic Sculpture, Sonoma State University Art Gallery, Rohnert Park, CA
1994	Shrines, Symbols and Cherished Objects, Fuller Museum of Art, Boston, MA
1992	Contemporary Uses of Wax & Encaustic, Palo Alto Cultural Center, Palo Alto, CA
1989	Surface and Form, The National Museum of Ceramic Art, Baltimore, MD

Fragile Blossoms Everson Museum of Art, Syracuse, NY
American Clay Artists, The Clay Studio, Philadelphia, PA

1987   American Ceramics Now: The twenty-seventh ceramic national exhibition,
        Everson Museum of Art, Syracuse, NY (traveled)
        The Eloquent Object, Philbrook Museum of Art, Tulsa, OK (traveled)

1986   American Potters Today, Victoria and Albert Museum, London, Great Britain
        Craft Today: poetry of the physical, American Crafts Museum, New York, NY

1985   Art in the San Francisco Bay Area, 1945-1980, Oakland Museum, Oakland, CA
        Recent Acquisitions, San Francisco Museum of Modern Art, San Francisco, CA

1984   The Dilexi Years, Oakland Museum, Oakland, CA

1983   California Clayworks: selections from the permanent collection, San Francisco Museum of Modern Art, San Francisco, CA
        Who's Afraid of American Pottery?, Museum Het Kruithuis, 's-Hertogenbosch, The Netherlands
        Ceramic Echoes: historical references in contemporary ceramics, Nelson-Atkins Museum, Kansas City, MO

1982   Twenty American Artists: sculpture 1982, San Francisco Museum of Modern Art, San Francisco, CA 1981
        Centering on Contemporary Clay, University of Iowa Museum of Art, Iowa City, Iowa
        A Century of Ceramics in the U.S, Everson Museum of Art, Syracuse, NY

1979   West Coast Ceramics, Stedelijk Museum, Amsterdam, The Netherlands

1977   A Decade of Ceramic art: 1962- 1972, San Francisco Museum of Modern Art, San Francisco,

1970   Objects: U.S.A, Smithsonian Institution, Washington D.C (traveled)

selected bibliography

• Catalogue of the Collection 1992. - Shigaraki: The Shigaraki Ceramic Cultural Park, 1993
• Ron Nagle: a survey exhibition 1958-1993 / essay Michael McTwigan. - Oakland: Mills College Art Gallery, 1993
• American Ceramics: the collection of Everson Museum of Art / ed. Barbara Perry. - New York: Rizzoli, 1989
• The History of American Ceramics: 1607 to the present, from pipkins and bean pots to contemporary forms / Elaine Levin. - New York: Harry N. Abrams, 1988
• American Ceramics: 1876 to the present / Garth Clark. - New York: Abbeville Press, 1987
• American Ceramics Now: twenty-seventh ceramic national exhibition. - Syracuse New York: Everson Museum of Art, 1987
• Clay Revisions: plate, cup, vase / Vicki Halper. - Seattle: Seattle Art Museum, 1987
• Painted Clay / text Jos Poodt. - 's-Hertogenbosch: Museum Het Kruithuis, 1987
• The New Ceramics: trends and traditions / Peter Dormer. - London: Thames and Hudson, 1986
• Ceramic Echoes: historical references in contemporary ceramics / ed. Garth Clark. - Kansas City: The Contemporary Art Society, 1983
• American Potters: the work of twenty modern masters / Garth Clark. - New York: Watson-Guptill, 1981
• Centering on contemporary clay: American ceramics from the Joan Mannheimer collection / texts Jim Melchert...et al. Iowa City: The University of Iowa Museum of Art, 1981
• Ron Nagle. - San Francisco: San Francisco Art Institute, 1978
• A Decade of Ceramic Art 1962-1972 / text Suzanne Foley. - San Francisco: San Francisco Museum of Art, 1972

GEORGE OHR
1857-1918

public collections

The Brooklyn Museum, Brooklyn, NY
Museum Het Kruithuis, 's-Hertogenbosch, The Netherlands
Missisippi Museum of Art, Jackson, MS
National Museum of History and Technology, Smithsonian Institute, Washington D.C.
The Newark Museum, Newark, NJ

selected exhibitions

1990   Museum Het Kruithuis, 's-Hertogenbosch, The Netherlands
1984   Garth Clark Gallery, New York, NY
1983   University of Mississippi (traveled)
1978   Mississippi State Historical Museum, Jackson, MS
1979   Bridgewater Mall, Gulfport, MS

selected bibliography

• The Mad Potter of Biloxi: the art and life of George E. Ohr / Garth Clark. - New York: Abbeville Press Publishers, 1989
• George E. Ohr: the mad Biloxi potter / Ron Dale. - Stamford: JO-D Books, 1983
• The Biloxi Art Pottery of George Ohr / text Garth Clark. - Mississippi: The Mississippi State Historical Museum, 1978

KEN PRICE
Born 1935

public collections

Art Institute of Chicago, Chicago, IL
Carnegie Museum of Art, Pittsburgh, PA
Dallas Museum of Art, Dallas, Dallas TX
Denver Art Museum, Denver, CO
Everson Museum of Art, Syracuse, NY
Hirshhorn Museum and Sculpture Garden, Washington, D.C.
Los Angeles County Museum of Art, Los Angeles, CA
Metropolitan Museum of Art, New York, NY
Minneapolis Institute of the Arts, Minneapolis, MN
Museum of Ceramic Art, Alfred University, NY
Museum of Contemporary Art, Los Angeles, CA
Museum of Modern Art, New York, NY
Museum Het Kruithuis, 's-Hertogenbosch, The Netherlands
National Gallery of Art, Washington, D.C.
Nelson-Atkins Museum of Art, Kansas City, MO
Renwick Gallery, National Museum of American Art, Smithsonian
Institution, Washington, D.C.
San Francisco Museum of Modern Art, San Francisco, CA
Seattle Art Museum, Seattle, WA
Stedelijk Museum, Amsterdam, The Netherlands
Victoria and Albert Museum, London, Great Britain
Whitney Museum of American Art, New York, NY

selected solo exhibitions

1998	Franklin Parrasch Gallery, New York, NY
1997	L.A. Louver Gallery, Venice, CA
1996	Franklin Parrasch Gallery, New York, NY
1995	Beaver College Art Gallery, Glenside, PA
1994	Harwood Foundation Museum of the University of New Mexico, Taos, MN
1992	Walker Art Center, Minneapolis, MN
	The Menil Collection, Houston, TX
1991	James Corcoran Gallery, Los Angeles, CA
1990	Sena West Gallery, Santa Fe, NM
1989	The Greenberg Gallery, St Louis, MO
	Rena Bransten Gallery, San Francisco, CA
1987	James Corcoran Gallery, Los Angeles, CA
1986	Fuller Goldeen Gallery, San Francisco, CA
1985	Willard Gallery, New York, NY
1984	Betsy Rosenfield Gallery, Chicago, IL
1983	Leo Castelli Gallery, New York, NY
1982	Santa Barbara Museum of Art, Santa Barbara, CA
1981	Contemporary Arts Museum, Houston, TX
1980	Visual Arts Museum, New York, NY
1979	Texas Gallery, Houston, TX
1978	Los Angeles County Museum of Arts, Los Angeles, CA
1976	The Greenberg Gallery, St. Louis, MO
1974	Felicity Samuel Gallery, London, Great Britain
1973	Galerie Neuendorf, Hamburg, Germany
1972	Fendrick Gallery, Washington, D.C.
1971	David Whitney Gallery, New York, NY
1970	Gemini G.E.I., Los Angeles, CA

selected group exhibitions

1998	Clay Into Art, The Metropolitan Museum of Art, New York, NY
1998	Biomorphic Abstraction, Curt Marcus Gallery, New York, NY
1997	Sunshine and Noir, Louisiana Museum of Modern Art, Humbleback, Denmark (traveled)
	Image, Plate, Vessel, Franklin Parrasch Gallery, New York, NY
1993	Contemporary Craft in the Saxe Collection, Toledo Museum of Art, Toledo, OH
	5 x 7, New York State College of Ceramics at Alfred University, Alfred, New York
1991	Selections from the Permanent Collection, Museum of Contemporary Art, Los Angeles, CA
	Shigaraki Ceramic Cultural Park, Shigaraki, Japan
1989	Kansas City Collects Contemporary Ceramics, Nelson-Atkins Museum of Art, Kansas City, MO
1987	Clay Revisions: cup, plate, vase, Seattle Art Museum, Seattle, WA
1984	A Different Climate, Städtische Kunsthalle, Düsseldorf, Germany
	Gemini G.E.L., Artand Collaboration, National Gallery of Art, Washington, DC
1982	Painting and Sculpture Today 1982, Indianapolis Museum of Art, Indianapolis, IN
1981	1981 Biennial Exhibition, Whitney Museum of American Art, New York, NY
	Ceramic Sculpture: 'six artists', Whitney Museum of American Art, New York, NY
1979	1979 Biennial Exhibition, Whitney Museum of American Art, New York, NY
	Contemporary Sculpture, The Museum of Modern Art, New York, NY
	West Coast Ceramics, Stedelijk Museum, Amsterdam, The Netherlands
1977	Small Objects, Whitney Museum of American Art, New York, NY
1976	200 Years of American Sculpture, Whitney Museum of American Art, New York, NY
1974	Clay, Whitney Museum of American Art, New York, NY
1972	West Coast, USA, Kolnischer Kunstverein, Cologne, Germany
	Joe Goode, Kenneth Price, Ed Ruscha, Museum Boijmans-van Beuningen, Rotterdam, The Netherlands
1971	Contemporary Ceramic Art, National Museum of Modern Art, Kyoto, Japan
1970	Contemporary American Sculpture, Whitney Museum of American Art, New York, NY

selected bibliography

• Ken Price: recent work. - New York: Franklin Parrasch Gallery, 1997
• Ken Price: a selected survey / Carter Ratcliff . - Glenside PA: Beaver College Art Gallery, 1995
• 5 x 7: seven ceramic artists each acknowledge: five sources of inspiration / Wayne Higby. - New York: Alfred University, 1993
• Ken Price / Walter Hopps. - Houston: Menil Foundation, 1992
• Clay Today: contemporary ceramists and their work / Martha Drexler Lynn. - Los Angeles: Los Angeles County Museum, 1990
• Ken Price / Jeff Perone. - New York: Charles Cowles Gallery, 1989
• The History of American Ceramics: 1607 to the present, from pipkins and bean pots to contemporary forms / Elaine Levin. - New York: Harry N. Abrams, 1988
• American Ceramics: 1976 to the present / Garth Clark. New York: Abbeville Press, 1987
• American Ceramics Now: twenty-seventh ceramic national exhibition. - Syracuse New York: Everson Museum of Art, 1987
• Clay Revisions: plate, cup, vase / Vicki Halper. - Seattle: Seattle Art Museum, 1987
• The New Ceramics: trends and traditions / Peter Dormer. - London: Thames and Hudson, 1986
• Ceramic Echoes: historical references in contemporary ceramics / Garth Clark. - Kansas City Missouri: The Contemporary Art Society, 1983
• American Potters: the work of twenty modern masters / Garth Clark. - New York: Watson-Guptill, 1981
• Ceramic Sculpture:'six artists'/ Richard Marshall and Suzanne Foley. - New York: Whitney Museum of American Art, 1981
• West Coast Ceramics: keramisch beeldhouwwerk uit de Verenigde Staten. - Amsterdam: Stedelijk Museum, 1979
• Nine West Coast Clay Sculptors: 1978. - Syracuse: Everson Museum of Art, 1978
• A Decade of Ceramic Art 1962-1972 / Suzanne Foley. - San Francisco: San Francisco Museum of Art, 1972

ADRIAN SAXE
Born 1943

public collections
Everson Museum of Art, Syracuse, NY
Los Angeles County Museum of Art, Los Angeles, CA
The Metropolitan Museum of Art, New York, NY
Musée des Arts Décoratifs, Pavallion de Marsan, Palais du Louvre, Paris France
Musée National de Céramique de Sèvres, Sèvres, France
Museum Het Kruithuis, 's-Hertogenbosch, The Netherlands
Museum of Art, Carnegie Institute, Pittsburg, PA
The Museum of Contemporary Ceramic Art, Shigaraki Ceramic Cultural Park, Japan
Nelson-Atkins Museum of Art, Kansas City, MO
Oakland Museum, Oakland, CA
Renwick Gallery, National Collection of American Art, Smithsonian Institution, Washington, DC

selected solo exhibitions
1998	Frank Lloyd Gallery, Los Angeles, CA
1997	Garth Clark Gallery, New York, NY
1995	Garth Clark Gallery, Los Angeles, CA
1993	Los Angeles County Museum of Art, Los Angeles, CA
1991	Garth Clark Gallery, Los Angeles, CA
1987	Art Gallery, University of Missouri, Kansas City, MO
1985	The American Hand, Washington, DC
1983	Garth Clark Gallery, New York, NY
	Thomas Segal Gallery, Boston, MA
1982	Garth Clark Gallery, Los Angeles, CA
1979	The American Hand, Washington, DC
1970	Canyon Gallery II, Los Angeles, CA

selected group exhibitions
1999	Art and Industry: Contemporary Porcelain from Sèvres, American Craft Museum, New York, NY
1998	Clay into Art, Metropolitan Museum of Art, New York, NY
1995	The White House Collection, National Museum of American Art, Smithsonian Institution, Washington, DC
1994	The Collector's Eye-Contemporary Ceramics: American, Canadian and British from the Collection of Aaron Milrad, The Koffler Gallery, Toronto, Canada
1993	Contemporary Crafts and the Saxe Collection, The Toledo Museum of Art, Toledo, OH
1991	Metamorphosis of Contemporary Ceramics, The Museum of Contemporary Ceramic Art, Shigaraki Ceramic Cultural Park, Japan
1990	Vessels from Use to Symbol, American Craft Museum, New York, NY
1989	Kansas City Collects Contemporary Ceramics, Nelson-Atkins Museum of Art, Kansas City, MO
1988	East-West Contemporary Ceramics, Art Center of Korean Culture

	and Arts Foundation, Seoul, Korea
	Création de la Manufacture de Sèvres: 1982-1987, Hall du CNAP, Paris, France
1987	American Ceramics Now, Everson Museum of Art, Syracuse, NY (traveled)
	The Eloquent Object, Philbrook Art Museum, Tulsa, OK (traveled)
	Quatre Americains à la Manufacture de Sèvres, American Center, Paris, France
1986	American Potters Today, Victoria and Albert Museum, London, Great Britain
1985	20th Century American Ceramics, Musée de Ceramica, Barcelona, Spain (traveled)
	Clay: Everyday plus Sunday, John Michael Kohler Arts Center, Sheboygan, WI
1984	Art in Clay: 1950's-1980's in Southern California, Municipal Gallery, Los Angeles, CA
1983	Ceramic Echoes: historical references in contemporary ceramics, Nelson-Atkins Museum of Art, Kansas City, MO
1982	Clay Choices by Clay Artists, Contemporary Crafts Association, Portland, OR
1981	Made in LA: Contemporary Crafts '81, Craft and Folk Art Museum, Los Angeles, CA
1980	American Porcelain: new expressions in an ancient art, Renwick Gallery, National Collection of American Art, Smithsonian Institution, Washington, DC (traveled)
1977	Ceramic Conjunction, Long Beach Museum of Art, Long Beach, CA
1971	Contemporary Ceramic Art: Canada, USA, Mexico, and Japan, The National Museum of Modern Art, Tokyo (traveled)

selected bibliography
• Contemporary Ceramics-Selections from the Metropolitan Museum of Art / Jane Adlin. - New York: The Metropolitan Museum of Art, 1998
• The Clay Art of Adrian Saxe / Martha Drexler Lynn .- Los Angeles: Los Angeles County Museum of Art, 1993
• Clay Today: contemporary Ceramists and their work / Martha Drexler Lynn. - Los Angeles: Los Angeles County Museum, 1990
• American Ceramics: The collection of Everson Museum of Art / ed. Barbara Perry. - New York: Rizzoli, 1989
• The Eccentric Teapot / Garth Clark. - New York: Abbeville Press, 1988
• Adrian Saxe / Peter Schjeldahl and Jeff Perrone. - Kansas City: The University of Missouri, 1987
• American Ceramics: 1876 to the present / Garth Clark.- New York: Abbeville Press, 1987
• American Ceramics Now: the twenty-seventh ceramic national exhibition / Syracuse, New York: Everson Museum of Art, 1987
• Quatre Americains à la Manufacture de Sèvres: exposition American Center. - Paris: American Center, 1987
• American Potters Today / Garth Clark and Oliver Watson . - London: Victoria and Albert Museum, 1986
• The New Ceramics: trends and traditions / Peter Dormer. - London Thames and Hudson, 1986
• Ceramic Echoes: historical references in contemporary ceramics / ed. Garth Clark. - Kansas City Missouri: The Contemporary Art Society, 1983
• Porcelain: traditions and new visions / Jan Axel and Karen McCready. - New York: Watson-Guptill, 1981

RUDOLF STAFFEL
Born 1911

public collections
Arkansas Arts Center, Little Rock, AR
Carnegie Museum of Art, Pittsburgh. PA
Los Angeles County Museum of Art, Los Angeles, CA
Museum Boijmans van Beuningen, Rotterdam, The Netherlands
Museum Het Kruithuis, 's-Hertogenbosch, The Netherlands
Museum of Fine Arts, Boston, MA
Philadelphia Museum of Art, Philadelphia, PA
Saint Louis Art Museum, St. Louis, MO
Shigaraki Ceramic Cultural Park, Shigaraki, Japan

selected solo exhibitions
1997   Museum of Art, Philadelphia, PA
1996   Taideteollisuusmuseo/ Museum of Applied Arts, Helsinki, Finland
1995   Helen Drutt Gallery, Philadelphia, PA
1991   Helen Drutt Gallery, Philadelphia, PA
1990   Museum Het Kruithuis, 's-Hertogenbosch, The Netherlands
1989   Temple Gallery, Temple University, Philadelphia. PA
1988   Helen Drutt Gallery, New York, NY
1985   Helen Drutt Gallery, Philadelphia, PA
1981   Helen Drutt Gallery, Philadelphia, PA
1976   Helen Drutt Gallery, Philadelphia, PA

selected group exhibitions
1994   The Ritual Vessel, Perimeter Gallery, Chicago, IL
1993   Contemporary Crafts and the Saxe Collection, Toledo Museum of
        Art, Toledo, OH
1992   From the Ground Up: ten Philadelphia clay artists, Goldie Paley
        Gallery, Philadelphia, PA
1989   National Objects Invitational, The Arkansas Arts Center
        Decorative Arts Museum, Little Rock, AR
        American Clay Artists, Port of History Museum, Philadelphia, PA
1988   Power Over the Clay: American studio potters, The Detroit
        Institute of Arts, Detroit, MI
1987   American Ceramics Now, Everson Museum of Art, Syracuse, NY
1986   Contemporary Arts: an expanding view, Monmouth Museum of
        Art, Lincroft, NJ
        Craft Today: poetry of the physical, American Craft Museum,
        New York, NY
        American Potters Today, Victoria and Albert Museum, London,
        Great Britain
1984   Directions in Contemporary American Ceramics, Museum of Fine
        Arts, Boston, MA
1983   American Clay Artists: Philadelphia 83, The Clay Studio,
        Philadelphia, PA
1981   Centering on Contemporary Clay, American ceramics from the
        Joan Mannheimer Collection, University of Iowa, Museum of Art,
        Iowa City IA
1980   American Porcelain: new expressions in American art, Renwick

Gallery of the National Museum of American Art, Smithsonian
Institution, Washington, DC
1979   A Century of Ceramics in the United States, Everson Museum of
        Art, Syracuse, NY
1976   Philadelphia: three centuries of American art, Philadelphia
        Museum of Art, Philadelphia, PA
1973   The Tyler Years/ Lechtzin, Staffel, Viesulas, Tyler School of Art,
        Elkins Park, PA
1972-73 Thirty Ceramics, Victoria and Albert Museum, London, Great
        Britain (traveled)

selected bibliography
• Rudolf Staffel: searching for light / text Marianne Aav. - Helsinki:
Taideteollisuusmuseo Museum of Applied Arts, 1996
• Catalogue of the collection 1992: The Shigaraki Ceramic Cultural Park. -
Shigaraki: The Shigaraki Ceramic Cultural Park, 1993
• From the Ground Up: ten Philadelphia clay artists / text Richard Torchia.
- Philadelphia: Goldie Paley Gallery, 1992
• An Industrious Art: innovation in pattern and print at the Fabric Workshop /
ed. Marion Boulton Stroud. - Philadelphia: The Fabric Workshop, 1991
• International Crafts / ed. by Martina Margetts. - London: Thames and
Hudson, 1991
• Clay Today: contemporary ceramists and their work / Martha Drexler
Lynn. - Los Angeles: Los Angeles County Museum, 1990
• Rudolf Staffel: transparency in clay / text Ivy L. Barski, Stephen Berg. -
's-Hertogenbosch: Museum Het Kruithuis, 1990
• American Ceramics: the collection of Everson Museum of Art / ed.
Barbara Perry. - New York: Rizzoli, 1989
• Craft Art: a collector's guide / Barbara Mayer. - Salt Lake City: Gibbs M.
Smith, Inc., 1988
• The History of American Ceramics: 1607 to the present, from pipkins
and bean pots to contemporary forms / Elaine Levin. - New York: Harry N.
Abrams, 1988
• American ceramics: 1876 to the present / Garth Clark. - New York:
Abbeville Press, 1987
• American ceramics now: twenty-seventh ceramic national exhibition. -
Syracuse New York: Everson Museum of Art, 1987
• The new ceramics: trends and traditions / Peter Dormer. - Londen:
Thames and Hudson, 1986
• Master Craftsmen: Wayne Higby, Jerry Rothman, Rudolf Staffel, Patti
Warashina. - Jacksonville: Art Museum, 1982
• American potters: the work of twenty modern masters / by Garth Clark. -
New York: Watson-Guptill, 1981
• Centering on contemporary clay: American ceramics from the Joan
Mannheimer collection / texts Jim Melchert...et.al. - Iowa City: The
University of Iowa Museum of Art, 1981
• American Porcelain: new expressions in an ancient art / Lloyd E. Herman.
- Oregon: Timber Press, 1980
• The contemporary American Potter: recent Vessels / essays Garth Clark
and Sanford Sivitz Shaman. - Cedar Falls: University of Northern Iowa,
1980
• A Century of Ceramics in the United States 1878-1978: a study of its
development / Garth Clark. - New York: Dutton, 1979

ROBERT TURNER
Born 1913

/ text Wayne Higby. - New York: Alfred University, 1993
• Clay Today: contemporary ceramists and their work / Martha Drexler Lynn. - Los Angeles: Los Angeles County Museum, 1990
• American Ceramics: the collection of Everson Museum of Art / ed. Barbara Perry. - New York: Rizzoli, 1989
• The New Ceramics: trends and traditions / Peter Dormer. - London: Thames and Hudson, 1986
• Ceramic Echoes: historical references in contemporary ceramics / ed. Garth Clark. - Kansas City Missouri: The Contemporary Art Society, 1983
• Who's afraid of American Pottery? / text Evert van Straaten...et al. - 's-Hertogenbosch: Museum Het Kruithuis, 1983
• The Contemporary American Potter: recent vessels / essays Garth Clark and Anford Sivitz Shaman. - Cedar Falls: University of Northern Iowa, 1980
• American Potters: the work of twenty modern masters / Garth Clark. - New York: Watson-Guptill, 1981
• The ceramic vessel as metaphor: sixth national ceramics invitational. - Evanston: Art Center, 1977

public collections
American Craft Museum, New York, NY
Everson Museum of Art, Syracuse, NY
Los Angeles County Museum of Art, Los Angeles, CA
Milwaukee Art Museum, Milwaukee, WI
Museum Het Kruithuis, 's-Hertogenbosch, The Netherlands
Museum of Fine Arts, Boston, MA
National Museum of Korea, Seoul, Korea
Nelson-Atkins Museum of Fine Arts, Kansas City, MO
Philadelphia Museum of Art, Philadelphia, PA
St. Louis Museum of Art, Saint Louis, MO

selected solo exhibitions

1992	Nora Eccles Harrison Museum of Art, Logan, Utah
1991	Dorothy Weiss Gallery, San Francisco, CA
1990	Bellas Artes Gallery, Santa Fe, NM
1989	Helen Drutt Gallery, New York City
1987	Garth Clark Gallery, New York City
	Dorothy Weiss Gallery, San Francisco, CA
1986	Helen Drutt Gallery, Philadelphia, PA
1985	Milwaukee Art Museum, Milwaukee, WI
1983	University of Winsconsin, Eau Claire, WI
1982	Exhibit A, Chicago, IL
1981	Okun- Thomas Gallery, St, Louis, MI

selected group exhibitions

1993	Celebrating Artistry in Craft: American Craft Council Gold Medal, American Craft Council, New York, NY
1992	DeVore, Turner, Woodman & Voulkos, Greenberg Gallery, St. Louis, MO
1990	The Greenberg Gallery: its clay artists, Greenberg Gallery, St. Louis, MO
1987	The Ritual Vessel, Twining Gallery, New York, NY
1986	Craft Today: poetry of the physical, American Craft Museum, New York, NY
	Contemporary Arts: an expanding view, Monmouth Museum of Art, Lincroft, NJ
1985	Histories: past, present and accounted, Exhibit A, Chicago, IL
1984	Direction in Contemporary American Ceramics, Museum of Fine Arts, Boston, MA
	Clay Vessels: Works by 10 Modern Masters, Palo Alto Cultural Center, CA
1983	Who's Afraid of American Pottery?, Museum Het Kruithuis, 's-Hertogenbosch, The Netherlands

selected bibliography
• Alfred teaches ceramics, 1900-1996 / compiled and ed. Margaret Carney. - New York: Museum of Ceramic Art at Alfred, 1996
• 5 x 7: seven ceramic artists each acknowledge: five sources of inspiration

PETER VOULKOS
Born 1924

public collections
American Craft Museum, New York, NY
Australian National Gallery, Canberra, Australia
Carnegie Museum of Art, Pittsburgh, PA
Denver Art Museum, Denver, CO
Des Moines Art Center, Des Moines, IA
Everson Museum of Art, Syracuse, NY
Los Angeles County Museum of Art, Los Angeles, CA
Metropolitan Museum of Art, New York, NY
Musée des Arts Decoratifs de Montreal, Montreal, Canada
Museum Boijmans van Beuningen, Rotterdam, The Netherlands
Museum Het Kruithuis, 's-Hertogenbosch, The Netherlands
Museum of Contemporary Ceramic Art, Shigaraki Ceramic Cultural Park, Japan
National Gallery of Art, Melbourne, Australia
National Museum of Modern Art, Kyoto, Japan
Nelson-Atkins Museum of Art, Kansas City, MO
San Francisco Museum of Modern Art, San Francisco, CA
Stedelijk Museum, Amsterdam, The Netherlands
Stedelijk Van Abbemuseum, Eindhoven, The Netherlands
Victoria and Albert Museum, London, Great Britain
Whitney Museum of American Art, New York, NY

selected solo exhibitions
1997	Perimeter Gallery, Chicago, IL
1996	Kenji Taki Gallery, Nagoya, Japan
1997	Oakland Museum, Oakland, CA
1995	Art Gallery of New South Wales, Sydney, Australia (traveled)
1993	Hordaland Kunstnerseentrum, Bergen, Norway (traveled)
1991	Braunstein/Quay Gallery, San Francisco, CA
1988	Twining Gallery, New York, NY
1986	Braunstein/Quay Gallery, San Francisco, CA
1985	Exhibit A, Chicago, IL
1984	Magnolia Gallery, Oakland, CA
1983	Art Center, Tokyo, Japan (traveled)
1982	Bruce Museum, Greenwich, CT
1981	Charles Cowles Gallery, New York, NY

selected group exhibitions
1998	NCECA 1998 Honors & Fellows Exhibition, Fort Worth Modern Art Museum, Fort Worth, TX
1996	Inter-Action: ceramic works by 7 artists, Kenji Taki Gallery, Nagoya, Japan
1996	Collection Highlights; 1945 to the present, Seattle Art Museum, Seattle, WA
1995	Made in America: ten centuries of American art, Minneapolis Institute of Arts, Minneapolis, MN (traveled)
1995	The Nude in Clay, Perimeter Gallery, Chicago, IL (traveled)
1995	Fifteen Profiles: distinguished California modernists, Fresno Art Museum, Fresno, CA
1994	Revolution in Clay: The Marer Collection of contemporary ceramics, Ruth Chandler Williamson Gallery, Scripps College, Claremont, CA (traveled)
1993	Celebrating Artistry in Craft: American Craft Council Gold Medal Recipients, Chicago Cultural Center, Chicago, IL
1990	Bay Area Sculptors of the 1960's: then and now, Braunstein/Quay Gallery, San Francisco, CA
1987	The Eloquent Object, Philbrook Museum of Art, Tulsa, OK (traveled)
1987	Clay Revisions: plate, cup, vase, Seattle Art Museum, Seattle, WA
1986	Craft Today: poetry of the physical, American Craft Museum, New York, NY (traveled)
1984	Art in Clay, Los Angeles Municipal Art Gallery, Los Angeles, CA
1983	Ceramic Echoes: historical references in contemporary ceramics, Nelson-Atkins Museum of Art, Kansas City, MO
1981	Ceramic Sculpture: 'six artists', Whitney Museum of American Art, New York, NY (traveled)
1979	A Century of Ceramics in the US, 1878-1978, Everson Museum of Art, Syracuse, NY (traveled)
1979	West Coast Ceramics, Stedelijk Museum, Amsterdam, The Netherlands
1978	Nine West Coast Sculptors: 1978, Everson Museum of Art, Syracuse, NY (traveled)
1974	Clay, Whitney Museum of American Art, New York, NY
1972	International Ceramics 1972, Victoria and Albert Museum, London, Great Britain
1972	A Decade of Ceramic Art, 1962-1972, San Francisco Museum of Art, San Francisco, CA
1970	Contemporary American Sculpture, Whitney Museum of Art, New York, NY

selected bibliography
• Peter Voulkos: retrospective. - Tokyo: Sezon Museum of Art, 1995
• Au-delà de la tradition: la collection de céramique contemporaine du Musée Boijmans-van Beuningen Rotterdam. - Paris: Institut Néerlandais, 1992
• International Crafts / ed. Martina Margetts. - London: Thames and Hudson, 1991
• Peter Voulkos. - San Francisco: Braunstein/Quai Gallery, 1991
• Clay Today: contemporary ceramists and their work / Marthe Drexler Lynn. - Los Angeles: Los Angeles County Museum, 1990
• American Ceramics: the collection of Everson Museum of Art / ed. Barbara Perry. - New York: Rizzoli, 1989
• American Ceramics: 1876 to the present / Garth Clark. - New York: Abbeville Press, 1987
• American Ceramics Now: twenty-seventh ceramic national exhibition / Syracuse New York: Everson Museum of Art, 1987
• The New Ceramics: trends and traditions / Peter Dormer. - London: Thames and Hudson, 1986
• Ceramic Echoes: historical references in contemporary ceramics / ed. Garth Clark. - Kansas City Missouri: The Contemporary Art Society, 1983
• Figurative clay sculpture Northern Californian / text Mady Jones. - San Francisco: Quai Gallery, 1982
• American Potters: the work of twenty modern masters / Garth Clark. - New York: Watson-Guptill, 1981
• Centering on contemporary clay: American ceramics from the Joan Mannheimer collection / text Jim Melchert…et.al. - Iowa City: The University of Iowa Museum of Art, 1981
• Ceramic Sculpture: 'Six Artists' / Richard Marshall and Suzanne Foley. - New York: Whitney Museum of American Art, 1981
• Nine West Coast clay sculptors: 1978. - Syracuse: Everson Museum of Art, 1978
• Peter Voulkos: a dialogue with clay / Rose Slivka. - New York: New York Graphic Society, 1978
• The Ceramic Vessel as Methaphor: sixth national ceramics invitational. - Evanston: Art Center, 1977
• Peter Voulkos: bronze sculpture. - San Francisco: Museum of Art, 1972

BETTY WOODMAN
Born 1930

public collections

Museum of Fine Arts, Boston, MA
Carnegie-Mellon Institute, Pittsburgh, PA
Cleveland Museum of Art, Cleveland, OH
Denver Art Museum, Denver, CO
Museum Het Kruithuis, 's-Hertogenbosch, The Netherlands
International Ceramic Museum, Faenza, Italy
Los Angeles County Museum of Art, Los Angeles, CA
Metropolitan Museum of Art, New York, NY
Philadelphia Museum of Art, Philadelphia, PA
The Saint Louis Museum of Art, St. Louis, MO
Victoria and Albert Museum, London, England

selected solo exhibitions

1998	PMMK, Museum voor Moderne Kunst, Oostende, Belgium
1997	Max Protetch, New York, NY
	Musée d' Art Contemporain, Dunkerque, France
1996	Stedelijk Museum, Amsterdam, The Netherlands
1995	Museo Internazionale delle Ceramiche, Faenza, Italy
1994	Mat Protetch, New York, NY
	Musée des Arts Décoratifs, Paris, France
1993	Museum Het Kruithuis, 's-Hertogenbosch, The Netherlands
	Gallerie Francesca Pia, Bern, Switzerland
1992	Institute of Contemporary Art, University of Pennsylvania, Pennsylvania, PA
1991	Max Protetch Gallery, New York, NY
1989	Museum of Modern Art, New York, NY
1988	Denver Art Museum, Denver, CO
	Rena Bransten, San Francisco, CA
1986	Max Protetch Gallery, New York, NY
1985	Freedman Gallery at Albright College, Reading, PA
1984	The Aspen Garden, Aspen Museum, Aspen, CO
1981	Helen Drutt Gallery, Philadelphia, PA
1980	Rochester Art Center, Rochester, MN

selected group exhibitions

1993	In Touch, Olympic Winter Games, Lillehammer, Norway
1992	The Ceramic Still Life, Garth Clark Gallery, New York, NY
	DeVore, Turner, Woodman & Voulkos, Greenberg Gallery, St. Louis, MO
1991	The Shigaraki Ceramic Cultural Park, Shigaraki, Japan
	The Abstract Vessel, Oriel Gallery, Cardiff, Great Britain
1990	Vessels from Use to Symbol, American Craft Museum, New York, NY
1989	Craft Today USA, Musée des Arts Decoratifs, Paris, France
1988	Power over the Clay: American studio potters, Detroit Art Institute, Detroit, MI
1987	American Ceramics Now: The twenty-seventh annual ceramic national, Everson Museum of Art, Syracuse, NY

	Quatre Americains à Sèvres, American Center, Paris, France
1986	American Potters Today, Victoria and Albert Museum, London, Great Britain
	Craft Today: The poetry of the physical, American Craft Museum, New York, NY
1985	Architectural Ceramics: eight concepts, American Craft Museum, New York, NY
1983	Ceramic Echoes: historical references in contemporary ceramics, Nelson-Atkins Museum of Art, Kansas City, MO
1980	For the Tabletop, American Craft Museum, New York, NY
	American Porcelain, Renwick Sculpture Gallery of the Smithsonian Institute, Washington, DC

selected bibliography

- Invitation: 10 artistes de la terre / texte Christian Skimao. - Frejus: Office du Tourisme de la culture et de l animation, 1998
- Betty Woodman: glass / text Françoise Guichon. - Marseille: Cirva, 1996
- 'Il giardino dipinto'e altre opere / testi Gian Carlo Bojani. - Faenza: Museo Internazionale delle Ceramiche, 1995
- Catalogue of the collection 1992: The Shigaraki Ceramic Cultural Park. - Shigaraki: The Shigaraki Ceramic Cultural Park, 1993
- 5 x 7: seven ceramic artists each acknowledge: five sources of inspiration / text Wayne Higby. - New York: Alfred University, 1993
- The Abstract Vessel: ceramics in studio / John Houston. - London: Bellew Publishing Company, 1991
- Garden of Delight: keramiekworkshop / text Ilse Nelis. - 's-Hertogenbosch: Akademie voor Kunst en Vormgeving, 1991
- International Crafts / ed. Martina Margetts. - London: Thames and Hudson, 1991
- Betty Woodman: Opera Selecta / text Peter Schjeldahl, Gert Staal. - 's-Hertogenbosch: Museum Het Kruithuis, 1990
- Clay Today: contemporary ceramists and their work / Martha Drexler Lynn. - Los Angeles: Los Angeles County Museum, 1990
- American Ceramics: the collection of Everson Museum of Art / ed. Barbara Perry. - New York: Rizzoli, 1989
- Contemporary American Craft Art: a collector's guide / Barbara Mayer. - Salt Lake City: Gibbs M. Smith, 1988
- The History of American Ceramics: 1607 to the present, from pipkins and bean pots to contemporary forms / Elaine Levin. - New York: Harry N. Abrams, 1988
- American Ceramics: 1876 to the present / Garth Clark. - New York: Abbeville Press 1987
- American Ceramics Now: twenty-seventh ceramic national exhibition. - Syracuse, New York, Everson Museum of Art, 1987
- Betty Woodman / ed. Sissy Thomas. - St. Louis: The Greenberg Gallery, 1987
- Clay Revisions: plate, cup, vase / Vicki Halper. - Seattle: Seattle Art Museum, 1987
- Painted Clay / text Jos Poodt. - 's-Hertogenbosch: Museum Het Kruithuis, 1987
- Quatre Americains à la manufacture de Sèvres. - Sèvres: American Center, 1987
- The New Ceramics: trends and traditions / Peter Dormer. - London: Thames and Hudson, 1986
- The Ceramics of Betty Woodman / text Jeff Perrone. - Reading: Freedman Gallery, 1985
- Ceramic Echoes: historical references in contemporary ceramics / ed. Garth Clark. - Kansas City: The Contemporary Art Society, 1983
- Who's afraid of American Pottery? / text Evert van Straaten...et al. - 's-Hertogenbosch: Museum Het Kruithuis, 1983
- American Potters: the work of twenty modern masters / Garth Clark. - New York: Watson-Guptill, 1981
- American Porcelain: new expressions in an ancient art / Lloyd E. Herman. Oregon: Timber Press, 1980
- Betty Woodman. - Rochester: Art Center, 1980

RHONDA ZWILLINGER
Born 1950

public collections
Delaware Art Museum, Wilmington, DE
Deutsches Schuhmuseum, Offenbach, Germany
The Groninger Museum, Groningen, The Netherlands
Museum Het Kruithuis, 's-Hertogenbosch, The Netherlands
Paterson Museum, Paterson, NY

selected solo exhibitions
1992	Galerie OZ, Paris, France
1989	Gracie Mansion Gallery, New York, NY
	Museum Het Kruithuis, 's-Hertogenbosch, The Netherlands
1988	Fahey/Klein Gallery, Los Angeles, CA
1987	Galerie Kaess-Weiss, Stuttgart, Germany
1986	Galleria Murnik, Milan, Italy
	Fondation Cartier, Paris, France
1985	P.S.1, Long Island City, NY
	Delaware Art Museum, Wilmington, DE
1983	Gracie Mansion Gallery, NYC
1982	Windows on White, NYC

selected group exhibitions
1990	American Dreams, American Extremes, Museum Het Kruithuis, 's-Hertogenbosch, The Netherlands
1989	Less is a Bore, Groninger Museum, Groningen, The Netherlands
	Dashboard Art, John Michael Kohler Art Center, Sheboygan, WI
1988	Recent Tendencies in Sculpture, Museum Boijmans- van Beuningen, Rotterdam
	Contemporary American Beadwork, John Michael Kohler Arts Center, Sheboygan, WI
1987	Contemporary Diptychs: The New Shape of Content, Whitney Museum of American Art at Fairfield County
	New, Used & Improved: art for the eighties, Robert Berman Gallery, Santa Monica, CA
1986	NYC: New York Delaware Art Museum, Wilmington, DE
	Benefit Auction, Milwaukee Art Museum, Milwaukee, WI
1985	Neo York, Center for Contemporary Art, Seattle, WA
	New York Art Now: correspondences, Laforet Museum, Tokyo, Japan
	Group Show, Barbara Farber Gallery, Amsterdam, The Netherlands
1984	East Village Scene, Institute of Contemporary Arts, Philadelphia, PA
	Painting and Sculpture Today, Museum of Art, Indianapolis, IN
	12 New York Women, Engstrom Gallery, Stockholm, Sweden
1983	Prints and Drawings for Collectors, Cleveland Contemporary Art Center, Cleveland, OH
1982	Joint Forces, Brooklyn Museum, New York, NY
	A More Store, Documenta Kassel, Germany

selected bibliography
• Die Verlassenen Schuhe / Sabine Schütz. - Bonn: Rheinisches Landesmuseum, 1993
• Alessandro Mendini and…La Fabrica estetica: 100% make up / ed. Dario Moretti. - Crusinallo: Alessi, 1992
• Less is a bore: exuberance now / ed. Marie Helene Cornips. - Groningen: Groninger Museum, 1989
• Rhonda Zwillinger: keep in touch / text Els Hoek. - 's-Hertogenbosch: Museum Het Kruithuis, 1989
• Century '87: today's art face to face with Amsterdam's past. - Amsterdam, 1987
• Contemporary Diptychs: divided visions. - New York: Whitney Museum of American Art, 1987
• Effetto placebo / text Renato Barilli. - Milano: Galleria Murnik, 1987
• New, Used & Improved: art for the eighties / Peter Frank. - New York: Abbeville Press, 1987
• Correspondences, NY. - Tokyo: Laforet Museum, 1985

Edited by

Yvònne G.J.M. Joris

Museum Het Kruithuis

's-Hertogenbosch, NL

Texts

Arthur C. Danto, NY

Janet Koplos, NY

Photography

George Adams Gallery p. 20

Tom Burckhardt p. 120 left

Terry A. Collins p. 121

Anthony Cuñha p. 130

Mieke A. Hille p. 127 left

Michael Honer p. 21

Simpson Kalisher p. 17 fig. 2

Peer van der Kruis p. 26-117, 135

David Lubarsky p. 118

Brian Oglesbee p. 125 right

Frank J. Thomas p. 16, 18

Biography/bibliography

Wil van Gils

Museum Het Kruithuis

Translations

Ted Alkins, Bertem, B

Design

Opera Ontwerpers, Breda, NL

(Ton Homburg, Marty Schoutsen)

Lithography

PlantijnCasparie Breda, NL

Printed by

PlantijnCasparie Breda, NL

Published by

Het Kruithuis, Museum of Contemporary Art

Citadellaan 7, 5211 XA 's-Hertogenbosch, NL

ISBN 90 6538 212 7